Home is Where the Start Is

Richard Hogan is a psychotherapist who specializes in working with families. He is from Cork and, after getting an English degree from University College Cork (UCC), he spent his early working life as a secondary-school teacher. His classroom experiences prompted him to retrain as a family psychotherapist.

Richard has been in practice for a decade and is clinical director of the Therapy Institute in Dublin. He appears frequently across Irish radio and TV as an authoritative and practical voice on mental health issues. His weekly *Irish Examiner* column, 'Learning Points', explores his progressive approach to mental health promotion.

Richard is the recipient of a Fulbright Award and is completing a PhD exploring the intersection between psychological models of the family and educational theory, with a particular focus on inclusion. His first book was *Parenting the Screenager* ('A must buy for any parent of a teenager', *Irish Times*).

Richard lives in Dublin with his family.

Home is Where the Start Is

How Your Family Made You, and How You Can Make Yourself Even Better

RICHARD HOGAN

PENGUIN BOOKS

PENGUIN BOOKS

UK | USA | Canada | Ireland | Australia
India | New Zealand | South Africa

Penguin Books is part of the Penguin Random House group of companies
whose addresses can be found at global.penguinrandomhouse.com.

Penguin
Random House
UK

First published by Sandycove 2023
Published in Penguin Books 2024
001

Copyright © Richard Hogan, 2023

The moral right of the author has been asserted

Typeset by Jouve (UK), Milton Keynes
Printed and bound in Great Britain by Clays Ltd, Elcograf S.p.A.

The authorized representative in the EEA is Penguin Random House Ireland,
Morrison Chambers, 32 Nassau Street, Dublin D02 YH68

A CIP catalogue record for this book is available from the British Library

ISBN: 978-0-241-99665-2

www.greenpenguin.co.uk

MIX
Paper | Supporting
responsible forestry
FSC
www.fsc.org FSC® C018179

Penguin Random House is committed to a
sustainable future for our business, our readers
and our planet. This book is made from Forest
Stewardship Council® certified paper.

To my wife and children – you give my life meaning

Contents

Introduction: The start is only the beginning   xi

    The need to understand   xiii

    My approach   xiv

    Writing the story   xvi

PART ONE: THE GENOGRAM   I

1. Finding the patterns in your life story   5

    What is a genogram?   5

    What you can learn from a genogram   6

    How to compile a genogram   7

PART TWO: HOW YOUR HOME LIFE SHAPES YOUR WORLD VIEW   11

2. Learning before you can speak – the power of attachment   17

    What is attachment?   17

    You are not a prisoner   23

3. How we learn – welcome to your brain!   26

    The function of memory   27

    The physical effects of memory   31

    The dangers of priming   34

    Instant negativity? Come in, I was expecting you   35

PART THREE: THE MAKING OF YOU – UNDERSTANDING YOUR FAMILY   39

4. Family dynamics   43

    Nuclear family   43

Single-parent family 46

Blended family 48

Same-sex family 49

Grandparent family 50

The lasting effect of family dynamics 51

5. Your position in the family 54

Youngest 54

The forgotten middle child 55

Eldest 56

Sibling rivalry 56

6. Personalities at play within the family 59

The 'Big Five' personality traits 60

1. Openness 61

2. Conscientiousness 63

3. Extraversion 67

4. Agreeableness 69

5. Neuroticism 71

PART FOUR: THE CHILD INSIDE THE ADULT 77

7. How you can get sacrificed for family balance 83

Living up to your label 83

8. The unforgettable lessons of fear 88

Hot and cold cognition 88

What does fear do to the body? 89

Fear is learned 91

9. Comfortably numb – the power of positive
feedback loops 94

Taking control of not having control is
what gives you control 96

Phobic behaviours 97

Breaking the loop 99

10. How you talk to yourself matters 101

The power of internalized beliefs 102

PART FIVE: ADDICTION, SEPARATION AND FAMILY 109
DYSFUNCTION

11. Addiction and the family 115

Living with stress 117

The vicious circle of fear-based behaviour 120

The long-lasting effects of family
dysfunction 121

The familiarity of dysfunction 123

12. Separation and exclusion 130

The curse of distrust 131

Feeling responsible 133

Parental alienation 134

Normative estrangement 136

PART SIX: NAVIGATING LOVE 139

13. The language of love 143

Speaking of positivity 143

Your love language 145

Your love style 148

14. The language of conflict 152

PART SEVEN: CHOOSING NEW LEGACIES AS A PARENT 159

15. Positive relations 163

Positive legacies 163

Negative legacies 165

Changing family legacies 169

Contents

PART EIGHT: THE SCIENCE OF THRIVING 173

16. What is happiness? 177
  Personality and happiness 178
  The brain and happiness 179
  Being authentic – the me you see 180
  What does unhappiness look like? 181
17. The key components of well-being 188
  Autonomy and agency 188
  Openness 191
  Connection 192
  Writing your own narrative 195
  Purpose/meaning 196
18. Break down your obstacles to happiness 198
  How we live in fear 199
  The four aspects of thriving 204

PART NINE: HOME IS WHERE YOU START FROM . . . 211
BUT IT DOESN'T HAVE TO BE WHERE YOU FINISH

19. Accept your past self, change your present self 217
  Your past self 217
  Forgive and let go 224
  Change your present self 226
20. Write your own life story 229

Epilogue: A last thought – almost zero 234
Acknowledgements 237
Notes 239

Introduction

The start is only the beginning

I was no more than sixteen years old when I decided I wanted to become a family therapist.

My parents agreed it would be good for me to see a psychiatrist because I had been in trouble in school and my mood was low. The idea of seeing a psychiatrist wasn't exactly unwelcome. On the contrary, I was quite happy to go because no one had ever asked what life was like for me. I had acted out throughout my educational career – a suspension here and a detention there – but my behaviour was simply punished, never understood. The idea of talking to a trained professional, with penetrating insights into what was going on in my life, intrigued me greatly. I had the notion that I'd be sprawled on a couch, pensively reflecting and recalling my early childhood traumas while an aged, tweed-clad expert jotted down my poignant ramblings. There'd be a lot of 'Fascinating!' and 'Wonderful!' as I elucidated all the difficulties I'd had to endure as a child. Well, that's what I imagined.

As I was sitting in the waiting room, trying to guess at what the priest with the monobrow had wrong with him, my mother leaned in to me and whispered, 'Don't tell him about Dad, because he knows him.' In that moment, as the door was opened to usher me into the room, Richard Hogan Family Therapist was born. I've never forgotten that feeling. I felt empty, utterly alone. In that one sentence, the responsibility for all the issues in my life was firmly located within me. It had nothing to do with the difficult environment I was navigating, nothing to do with the ecology I came from. Nothing to do with the fact my father was an abusive alcoholic. Just me.

The meeting was nothing like I'd imagined. The psychiatrist was quick to inform me what a wonderful writer my father was (he wrote for the *Irish Times*) and then proceeded to ask very rudimentary questions about my family. He seemed to know the answers before I even responded. Not that I was my garrulous self, I was monosyllabic. His verdict, depression. His answer, Prozac.

My depression would deepen over the next few years as I discovered the true extent of my father's betrayals. Living with him meant living in a constantly changing, unpredictable environment. One moment everything functioned normally, the next he was falling in the door aggressively drunk and looking for a fight. It was a very insecure environment to grow up in. At times, I struggled to make sense of it.

Yet I never felt as hopeless and powerless as I did that day, as a teenager, sitting in front of that psychiatrist. His prescribing of Prozac still troubles me to this day. Medication wasn't going to change my reality. Well, maybe it would. It might have numbed my interactions with my environment, but my environment wasn't going to change. Medication wasn't going to change the fact that my father was an abusive alcoholic. That reality would still be there, waiting for me, even with medical intervention. That whole encounter planted the seed of my future self: I was determined to become a psychotherapist and help others.

As I look back on that time now, I know it was a lot to go through for a young boy. But it didn't really feel like I was living with abuse. It was my reality. And it made me strong. Resilient. I felt I could face difficult people and not bend to their will. I had been bullied by my father, but I had never shown him I was scared. I was, of course, but I stood up to him, and he wouldn't have thought I was scared. He would probably have said I was a tough kid. But I was very soft, too – I never wanted to hurt anyone in my life.

Living in dysfunction changes the way you think and how you see the world. It changes how you talk to yourself. It took me a considerable amount of time to work out a lot of my own experiences as a child. And that child is always with me, speaking to me when I'm talking with a teenager who is going through a turbulent time. That moment, waiting to see the psychiatrist, has replayed on a loop in my mind many times throughout my life. It has become one of those transformative moments we sometimes have. My road to Damascus. And the genesis of this book.

I remember reading the psychotherapy textbooks, as a student, and seeing the theory behind 'the identified patient'. The literature suggested that often the presenting patient manifests the pathology of the entire family. That was certainly me. I have worked with so many families over the years who have brought a child to the clinic, but in reality the child is bringing the family for help. I had the same thought sitting in the psychiatrist's office that morning. *Maybe this will be the help we all need?* But I felt utterly helpless at the end of that encounter. If a trained professional was blinded by the veneer of my father's status, I felt we were all doomed. Stuck, endlessly repeating the same patterns. That was a profoundly hopeless feeling to experience at such a young age.

The reason I am sharing this very personal story about my own life in such a public manner is because, too often, 'experts' present themselves as perfect. I am not perfect. I did not come out of a perfect home. I came out of a challenging home. A loving home in many ways, with a mother who was loving, caring and did her best, a father who was talented, angry and an addict, a grandmother who loved us and was great fun, and siblings who supported and tormented each other in equal measure. It was messy. Families are messy. People are very messy. There is no such thing as 'perfect'. That's why this book will offer you real examples, from real people, dealing with real-life situations. It is rooted in my own family experiences and in the experiences of hundreds of families and individuals who have sat with me and talked about their lives. It's all real.

The need to understand

Psychology had always been a passion of mine, growing up. Even before I encountered that psychiatrist when I was a teenager, I had long been fascinated by human behaviour and what made people tick. This early love of psychology re-emerged in my late twenties, and I started to think about going back to college and retraining. I was an English teacher at the time, and I loved my job, but this idea wouldn't leave me alone. I didn't want to leave anything unexplored. I wanted to test and push myself, to see what I was capable of. I had seen at first hand the impact of not doing that in my own father's life. His self-limiting beliefs were so visible, and they tainted everything. He wanted to be a writer but lacked the belief that he could be. He would tell us how he had ripped up a novel he had written – punctuating the story with how good the lost novel was.

I didn't want that to be me. I wanted to have the courage to strive, and I wanted to help other teenagers who'd been through something similar to my experience. That was the genesis of my interest in family, or 'systemic' psychotherapy, and it motivated me to change direction.

To this day, the kid I was back then, sitting in the psychiatrist's chair, is always with me in my clinic. Always talking to me about the family I am working with. Telling me never to assume an understanding of what is going on, but to remain curious and to ask questions.

My approach

I am a systemically trained family psychotherapist. The systemic approach to psychotherapy means that when a client comes to me for help, I consider their relationships with all the important systems in their life: family, friends, work, themselves, et cetera. None of us develops in isolation, we all come through incredibly dense and complicated systems to arrive at the person we are today. We are constantly functioning in an interconnected, reciprocal relationship with those around us. Family therapy analyses the problems people experience within the context of those systems of relationships. It examines the network of influences that impact all of us, and considers how those influences shape the story we tell ourselves about who we are. It uses the widest possible perspective.

In this book I will be describing the invisible forces that drive our lives, and the impact they have on our ability to authentically thrive and become who we know we were born to be. The genogram – the visual illustration of your family system – is one of the most important tools a systemic family therapist utilizes in their work. It will be an important part of the journey we go on together in this book.

Your family of origin, your relationship with your primary

caregiver, where you came in the family system, the labels given to you from that system and wider social system, your personality traits, your inner monologue, your relationship with family and friends, your internalized standard for happiness will all be discussed. I will offer you new ways to think about all of those aspects of your life. I will use case studies to illustrate the points being made and to show you how you can adopt better thinking habits. Physical habits and mental habits should be regarded in a similar way. We are intentional about going for a run or to the gym, but we rarely think about *how* we think and *why* we think a certain way. This book is designed to disrupt your thinking patterns and to present you with new ways of thinking that will allow you to live in a more positive and productive way.

All research points to the fact that this is the only life you will ever live. What would it be like to live that unique life in a more fearless way? What would it be like to thrive? That can often be a fear-provoking concept. We have struggled with insecurity, low self-esteem, anxiety and low mood for so long, it can become familiar, expected. This book endeavours to push you towards better thinking, better relationships with yourself, with your family and friends, while exploring the influences that shaped who you are today.

We all have the choice to become who we want to be, but first we must become aware of the invisible forces that drive our thoughts, feelings and behaviours. We must examine the behaviours that were modelled for us by our parents, but which are no longer working for us. We must discover which ones we subconsciously assimilated and which are now dominating our interactions and ruining our joy, so that we can start to live as our authentic self.

In my clinical experience, I meet two selves. The first self is drenched in self-doubt and self-criticism, drowning in all the negative labels it has heard over the years. The other self is the authentic self, unrestricted by role-modelling, family, labelling, attachments. It is free from the constraints of environment. The first self disrupts the progress of the second self. This book will allow that first self to articulate its presence, while empowering the second self to take control and become the more powerful of the two.

Writing the story

This book has brought me on a personal journey. That's the fascinating thing about writing, you never really know where it will take you. I didn't set out to talk about my own experience growing up. I wanted this to be a journey of awakening for the reader. But as I wrote, my own experience kept emerging, and rather than ignore it, I decided to embed it into the narrative of this book. I'm asking you to look back on your story, to review it honestly, to see the patterns that have permeated your life. In order to help you do that, I share my story with you in turn. The book isn't simply an examination or overview from a professional standpoint, it is also a deeply personal reflection on dysfunction in families, on living with addiction, on failing – again and again – before finally finding the way out and through, at last able to make peace with the past and, in doing so, be freed from it. I hope my own story helps you in understanding yours.

Home is where our start is, but it isn't where we end. That is up to us. We are not what happened to us but who we choose to become, and becoming is the most remarkable journey we will ever embark on. By undertaking the work set out here, by compiling your genogram (explained fully in Part One) and by engaging fully with all the layers of your own story, you get to decide what the next chapters will be.

We had very little control as children and adolescents, but now we are adults. That means we are our own authors. We get to write our own story.

PART ONE

The Genogram

I ONCE CARRIED OUT A PIECE OF RESEARCH ON MY ENTIRE FAMILY when I was a teenager, trying to find out what made them tick. The title of this study was 'Prolonged Teasing and Taunting'. I was basically trying to discover my brothers' trigger points and how many negative stimuli would be required before they reacted. My mother and grandmother were also a part of the sample cohort. However, my grandmother was militantly obtuse and skewed the findings. The study ended one morning when my eldest brother had enough and we got into a physical fight. I was left with a black eye, but some interesting data, too.

I loved listening to people's stories. I used to record my grand-mother telling stories about her life growing up in Ireland in the 1920s. I always enjoyed the company of older people, hearing their memories and analysing the moments when something significant happened.

As an adult, in my twenties, I taught English. The environment I created in my classroom was one where students could talk about their home lives. I knew that to get the best from a student, under-standing the curriculum was only part of the story. My students started talking to me about things that were happening in their lives, and that was what motivated me to find out more about fam-ily therapy – I wanted to understand the theory and science behind those conversations.

Our internal self-talk is the product of our relationship with the systems within which we developed. What we say and do impacts on the other person in a conversation, and their response to what we said or did to them impacts on our response, back and forth, and so the dance of intricate human communication goes. Every-one in the family system impacts on each other.

I wanted to figure out what was going on with myself, too. I wanted to get my head right and work through my childhood and be a better person. I was ready to take the first steps towards under-standing the family system in which I'd been raised. But first, I needed to compile a visual representation – a genogram.

1. Finding the patterns in your life story

What is a genogram?

The genogram was developed in the 1980s, by Monica McGoldrick and Randy Gerson, in family therapy and clinical psychology settings. They developed it for use as a tool in family therapeutic conversations. I use it every day in my clinic. Clients always comment on how significant they find it in helping them to understand the complex dynamic of their relationships.

The genogram is simply a drawing showing the connections between you and the people in your family, past and present. There is an example on page 8. Because of how you draw it – which I will explain on page 7 – you can see, pulled together visually in one place, all the dynamics of the family you and your parents grew up in. It can give you surprising insights into the invisible forces that motivated your parents and impacted how they parented you, which in turn shaped who you are today. Genograms show you any intergenerational patterns (patterns of behaviour repeated through family generations) that might be impacting your current relationships, while also showing any relevant psychological and medical issues present in the family. Once you understand how to draw your own genogram, you start the process of unearthing hidden familial patterns that are woven through your life. I will ask you to go back to your genogram and add more to it over the course of this book, to give you a broad insight into your family system and its effect on you.

A genogram differs from a family tree in that it is an interactive visual representation of a person's family relationships and history. It is interactive because the family system is never static. It is in a constant state of flux, a work-in-progress. The genogram is rarely drawn the same way twice, because family dynamics are continually moving and shifting. People often think, *Sure, I know my family history*. But it isn't until it is clearly drawn out in front of them that they begin to see the patterns emerge. It is always a striking moment in any therapeutic conversation.

Personally, I find doing the genogram very helpful in my life. I compile one annually because it illuminates changes that have taken place in my own family, and what changes remain to be made. I can track my behaviour and see where adjustments need to be made for the good of my family and myself. It's like an ongoing self-audit. The genogram helps me to gauge my levels of happiness and unhappiness, allowing me to then make choices that enable me to feel good about my life. It's an easy exercise that delivers so many benefits.

What you can learn from a genogram

Drawing your genogram is the most important task I am going to ask you to do. We will return to your genogram at the end of each chapter, to help you rethink your relationship with your family in light of what you've just read. As your understanding of your family of origin deepens, your genogram will become more detailed. This will be the foundation on which your understanding of yourself and your family will stand. We will build it together, piece by piece.

The genogram allows for all the unconscious internalized beliefs, values and behaviours that impact our lives to be seen clearly. Once we become aware of those values and beliefs, we can start to modify or erase any we feel are unhelpful in our lives.

In Chapter 13 ('The language of love') I will ask you to draw your partner's genogram. You might need to ask them for some information in order to get the detail you need; going back two generations will suffice. You will be looking at their family of origin while also filling in what their early attachments were like, their personality traits, the love language they speak (discussed in Chapter 13) and the intergenerational patterns present in their family. You will learn how they were parented and what they learned from growing up in their parents' relationship, which might explain why they react a certain way when they are pushed out of their comfort zone. Once we start to see all of those aspects, we begin to view the person in their entirety. It is much more difficult to reduce a person to narrow terms when we can see the complexity in their life and why they act the way they do.

The invisible forces that drive us will emerge from the swamp of the past. None of us is just here, in the present; we are all the product of a long history that stretches back through time. The genogram will bring to life the most immediate influences on your life and help you to see what needs to happen to allow you to become who you know you were meant to be.

How to compile a genogram

Don't be daunted by this process. It's actually quite simple when you get down to it. There are just a few easy steps to follow, and you will have a very clear visual representation of your family of origin.

You can start by drawing up your familiar family tree, showing names, dates of birth and death, marriages. This charts the generations in your family and their basic make-up. You could add in relevant medical information – such as premature deaths, addictions, death by suicide, stillbirths, et cetera. On to this basic 'map' of your family of origin, you can then add symbols to show the nature of the various relationships. For this you can use these simple symbols.

Square = male
Circle = female
Wavy line between people = conflict
One straight line through wavy line = conflicted separation
Two straight lines through wavy line = conflicted divorce
Four short lines through male or female = deceased
Thick wavy line between people = violence present in
  relationship

When compiling a genogram, the youngest should be on the right, moving towards the eldest on the left.

Here's a simple case study to show you how this works in practice.

CASE STUDY
History repeating

Mia came to see me because she had recently broken up with her boyfriend. She was in despair because she felt she always dated the wrong type of guy, and her recent relationship had ended after her boyfriend hit her – again. She explained that she felt very low all the time and her self-esteem was non-existent. She felt she deserved to be with men who didn't respect her; she never chose men who treated her well. There was a considerable amount of self-loathing apparent in our first conversation. Mia felt stuck and unsure if she would ever find happiness in her life. Together, we compiled her genogram.

In her genogram it became obvious that Mia had grown up in a dysfunctional household. Her father, Dan, had died (indicated by the four short lines in the box) from alcoholism. He and her mother, Mary, had a conflicted relationship (indicated by the wavy relational line between their names) and had eventually divorced (indicated by the two lines going through the wavy relational lines). Going a generation back, the genogram also shows details of Dan and Mary's families: Dan's parents, Ger

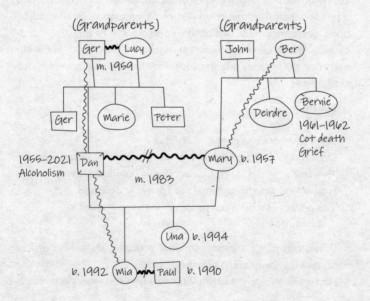

and Lucy, and his siblings, Ger, Marie and Peter; Mary's parents, John and Ber, and siblings, Deirdre and Bernie.

Now we can see a pattern of violence in two generations (indicated by the thickness of the wavy relational lines). Mia's father, Dan, grew up in a household where there was physical violence between his parents. And, in turn, there was violence between him and Mia's mother, Mary. Another interesting bit of information that emerged in doing the genogram is that Mary's sister, Bernie, died suddenly as a baby, so that would have been a source of trauma in her family. Clearly, Mia's parents came into their marriage carrying a lot of emotional baggage.

As Mia looked at this simple and short genogram, she started to see a pattern emerge. Her mother had married an addict and had been beaten up by him. Mia had grown up watching this and was replicating it in her adult life. Her relationship with her father was conflicted (indicated by the wavy line between them). She started to see, from looking at her genogram, that she was stuck seeking out familiar dysfunctional relationships. She was re-enacting her parents' relationship. They, in turn, had likely re-enacted patterns from the families they grew up in. Freud calls this the 'compulsion to repeat', and it is a powerful loop that children of dysfunction can easily become caught up in. Mia looked at her genogram and said, 'I wish I had done this when I was in my teens, it could have prevented a lot of pain.'

In our conversations she described a childhood of chaos and dysfunction. She explained that whenever things were going well for her, she did something to upset that peace. I have heard this so many times in my clinic. But sitting there that evening, staring at a simple genogram of her family – seeing family relationships laid out graphically over generations – Mia saw it all: the pattern that she was caught up in, and the desire to stay in chaos rather than choose to live in unfamiliar peace. When she saw the patterns presented like this, not only was she able to see clearly for the first time but – crucially – she was able to recognize and to accept what was happening and why.

—

The function of the genogram here is to help you clarify your thoughts as you read each chapter, and to reflect on if and how the issues raised resonate in your own life. The symbols are a handy short cut for key patterns, but you can also write words to describe the key patterns and information that are relevant to your life.

I won't be giving you a dense set of instructions for your genogram, or rigid rules for how to do it. I want you to understand its basic use – to set out patterns and give insights – and then you can compile your own genogram as suits you. Try to keep it simple – that way, you're far more likely to compile it, revise it regularly and benefit from it.

I'll give you prompts at the end of each chapter, to help you focus on what you need to think about and add to your genogram. In this way, step by step, you will gradually compile a diagram of your family and your life, giving you a broad perspective by the time you turn the last page.

PART TWO

How Your Home Life Shapes Your World View

WHEN I LOOK BACK ON MY EARLY LIFE, I CAN CLEARLY SEE THE frightened little boy who was trying to make sense of the world around him. You wouldn't have noticed to look at me that I was frightened. In fact, if you'd observed me, you would have thought I was unaware of what was going on. I would have seemed carefree, wild, running around the Grange Erin estate where I lived with my friends and then, as an adolescent, hanging out down in Maryborough in Cork. Getting into trouble, lost in the extravagances of youth. No stranger to the odd physical altercation. That's what I portrayed to the world. Some of it was true. But there was another reality.

During my adolescence I became depressed. There was constant fighting at home, the uncertainty of the emotional environment, a bowl hitting the wall because the dinner was too hot, screaming at night, not knowing who I'd meet in the morning. Embarrassment in front of the neighbours. The fun I had with my grandmother. The love I felt for my mother. And at times the conversations about The Beatles with my father. It was all a little confusing and unsettling. The house could be such fun, with singing and laughing and nice food, and then suddenly descend into chaos and aggression. It was very hard to process the inconsistent messages I was receiving. I still remember the tension I felt each time I walked up the hill into Grange Erin – I'd stand on my tippy-toes to see if the car was there or not – and the sinking feeling that would engulf me as I realized my father was home early. To this day, those memories still make me shiver.

It was the constant tension that was the most difficult thing to deal with. I could usually handle the outbreaks of violence or aggression, but the constant, simmering, unspoken tension was there every day. It is hard to articulate, but it changes you, it makes you uneasy at home. I still get that feeling sometimes, and it is incredibly unpleasant. It's as if there is a stranger in the house, a malevolent presence lurking somewhere. I have heard clients describe the same feeling when talking about their early childhood traumas. It haunts you.

What I have noticed over the years is that children who grow up with abuse or dysfunction often find it problematic to endure peace. And I use the word 'endure' purposely. Peace is something so alien to them, it is uncomfortable. I certainly felt that, for many years after I moved away from home.

Why is this?

What can happen is that the brain orients itself, in those early difficult years, to a heightened sense of threat and then exists in a permanent state of alert. When it experiences peace, that feels 'wrong', and the brain disrupts it by causing disharmony in order to get back to what is familiar. I had a client who once told me, 'I don't know what it is but sometimes when things are going good, I can hear myself saying, do something crazy.' This was the voice Mia heard, as we saw in the case study in the previous chapter. It is the voice that pushes you towards the familiar chaos.

What we experience in childhood, even when we are pre-verbal, is recorded in the brain and sets up expectations about the world and how it will behave towards us. For this reason, a traumatic childhood can impact people in myriad ways. It can make a vulnerable child come to view others as objects over which they can exert their influence and enjoy absolute power. They run a very destructive logic: 'Because this happened to me, I'm going to do this to you.' I often find this type of logic present in people who coercively control their partners. When we live with threat and are constantly alert as children, it affects our thinking and reasoning as adults. It can cause huge difficulties in our relationships as a result. On the flip side, it can also motivate us to pull ourselves out of that mindset and strive to improve. That did eventually happen for me, but it took some time. First, I needed to change how I viewed myself.

I often meet clients who are puzzled as to why they are being disingenuous with people. They are confused as to why they are not more authentic in their interactions. As we explore their emotions and examine their genogram, it becomes obvious that their attachments to their primary caregiver were insecure and caused them to constantly shift their behaviours in order to survive. When we do this in the early stages of our development, it can have huge consequences in our adult life. We know we are shape-shifting to suit our boss or manager or spouse, and we start to resent ourselves for the way we are behaving, because we know it isn't our true self we are presenting to the world. But we don't know why we are doing it. That can cause an incredible amount of pain and suffering. Those early attachments are so significant in our later relationships. How we experienced care in those months and years of early development are always present in our current interactions.

My early childhood experiences formed my perception of myself: I felt incredibly powerless. For anyone living with tension and chaos, it can deplete your reservoir of hope. And hope is such an important thing to have as a human being. That is why it's essential to dig down into your earliest experiences in life and to become aware of the foundations laid down for you before you had conscious choice.

2. Learning before you can speak – the power of attachment

What is attachment?

The concept of early childhood attachment types was first put forward by psychoanalyst John Bowlby in the 1950s. Attachment theory explains how your bond with your primary caregiver in childhood sets the foundation for the way you navigate relationships throughout your life.

Attachment theory holds that the fundamental goal of a human infant is to maintain proximity to its caregiver. This primal instinct goes all the way back to the early times of our evolution as a species, when not connecting with a caregiver meant certain death for the infant. This primary goal means that infants are constantly processing the dynamics of their relationship with their caregiver and developing strategies to stay close to them.

The key here is how the caregiver responds to this primary need in the infant. If that bond was disrupted or negative, you will struggle in adult life to make or maintain healthy bonds with those you love. Attachment happens, or doesn't happen, when you are pre-verbal and unable to consciously process it, yet it can continue to affect you throughout your life. The attachment style you experienced lays down a world model – a set of expectations about how the world behaves and responds to you – and this model influences you for life.

There are four types of attachment.

- Secure
- Avoidant
- Anxious
- Disorganized

Secure attachment

Secure attachment occurs when a child feels safe, loved, validated and able to express themselves without fear of recrimination or judgement. A child who develops in this type of environment learns that they can take risks and be themselves. They are not fearful of expressing themselves and, more importantly, they do not change who they are to suit the person they are with. They are comfortable in their own skin and can handle when people do not like them. They are not constantly looking for reassurance.

People with a secure attachment style are:

- able to regulate their emotions
- trusting
- good communicators
- comfortable in their own company
- able to self-reflect
- emotionally available and can handle uncertainty.

Avoidant attachment

If your parents were emotionally unavailable or distant, you may find it difficult to create solid and deep emotional bonds with people in your adult life. In my clinical experience, if parents are autocratic in their parenting style, it can cause a child to struggle with their emotional self.

If children experience their parents as uninterested or uncaring, this causes them to rely on themselves more than their caregiver for emotional support. They realize very quickly that they must learn to control their feelings, because feelings are not validated within this family dynamic. Emotions disrupt the balance of the family and are therefore denied. Did your parents leave you to fend for yourself? Did they criticize you for needing them? Did they reject any display of emotion from you? Did they ignore your basic emotional needs?

If you have developed an avoidant attachment style, you will:

- avoid emotional or physical intimacy
- find the expression of emotions difficult

- be dismissive of other people's emotions
- find trusting people very difficult
- be distrustful of anyone who attempts to get close to you
- be almost pathologically independent, to the point where you don't allow people into your life.

We all need emotional intimacy in order to thrive, but this ability to connect emotionally appears to be significantly lower in a person who has experienced this type of attachment with their caregiver. I have met this type of person so many times in my clinic, particularly in couples therapy. It is not gender-specific, but it can cause huge problems for the couple as one partner constantly feels they are being kept at arm's length by the other. They may feel like there is an impenetrable wall between them and their partner, and they may struggle to connect with them in any meaningful way. If you were never taught as a young child how to forge emotional connections, it is very difficult to learn how to do so in later life.

Anxious attachment

This type of attachment style arises when parenting is inconsistent and doesn't take the child's needs into consideration. Inconsistent messages are very destructive for a child's development and can have a significant negative effect on your ability to function in adult life. Children who grow up in this type of environment find it almost impossible to understand their caregiver. Communication is confusing and they feel incredibly unstable. There is nothing certain in this type of attachment; the child finds it impossible to calibrate their surroundings because the ground is constantly changing beneath their feet.

When I work with anxious children and adults, this early attachment is frequently at the root of their current anxiety. I often think anxiety is like having a map of the road ahead, but with some key features missing, so you don't have all the information you need to successfully complete the journey. This provokes both an emotional and a physiological response. When you grow up with an anxious style of attachment, it erodes the map and leads you to believe that you do not have the skills to manage any future life event. That causes huge anxiety.

The most confusing thing about this attachment style for children is that they experience very high levels of distress when their caregiver leaves. Such children tend to have strong emotional responses to separation. This is because they have learned that their caregiver is unpredictable and capable of change in any given moment, which causes a deep desire to be close to them at all times. If the caregiver leaves, will they ever come back? It's impossible to be sure.

I once worked with a young teenager whose mother had entered into a new relationship and brought him into a blended family. It was extremely clear that the messages she was giving her son were confusing. He didn't particularly relate to his stepfather, so he spent most of his time in his bedroom. In my conversations with the mother, I struggled to understand what she was trying to say. She spoke in long, dense tirades that were nearly impossible to decipher. When I spoke to them together, I could see that her son was anxious, that he believed there was something wrong with him for not being able to grasp what his mother was telling him. When I asked her to explain what she meant, and in more succinct language, she spoke to me like I was a confused little child – and I was still none the wiser.

When I asked her to repeat the message she wanted her son to hear, she said, 'I need him to be better than he has been and no better than that. I don't want him to be perfect, that would be nice, but he has to be better because we can't go on with him like the way he is, demanding like his father, and happy in his own company. I didn't realize how annoyed I am about it all, gosh, I am annoyed, I need him to just be better, I don't think that is too much to ask for.' When I asked her to clearly describe what 'better' would look like, she became irritated and said, 'Do I have to explain every little thing to you, my dear boy?'

There is a process in family therapy called 'isomorphism', whereby the therapist gets to experience what the client is experiencing through their interactions. I felt it in that moment. I could see her son look at me in a knowing way, and I could see the pressure on his shoulders lift. He realized that it wasn't him.

You likely experienced this type of attachment as a child if you had parents who:

- were easily overwhelmed
- made you responsible for how they felt
- could be incredibly attentive and then at other times push you away and disconnect from you.

A huge consequence of experiencing this attachment style as a child is that as an adult you believe you are responsible for how other people feel and often become co-dependent, needing constant reassurance from others. The more reassurance you receive, the more you need, and the more you need, the more you seek it out. This can make it very difficult to sustain healthy relationships.

The signs of an anxious attachment style are:

- being highly sensitive to criticism (real or perceived)
- seeking and needing constant approval from others
- jealous tendencies
- being very needy and co-dependent
- feeling unworthy of love
- intense fear of rejection
- significant fear of abandonment
- difficulty trusting others
- an internal negative voice.

Ultimately, a person who has experienced this in their early development will usually develop a deep-rooted fear of being abandoned, rejected, or alone. This will often cause them to become a pleaser. The more they do for others, the more valuable they believe they are – a belief that can really spiral into suffering in adult life. Eventually, they realize they cannot sustain this persona. They can end up resenting those who position them as pleasers, and resenting themselves for not having the strength to say no when they don't want to do something.

Disorganized attachment

The most common cause of a disorganized attachment is early child-hood trauma, neglect or abuse. The child in this situation experiences a profound conflict, because their parents are often the source of both their comfort and their fear; these contradictory feelings coexist with regard to the primary caregiver. It is this sense of confusion and uncertainty that gives rise to disorganized behaviours.

Research has shown that this type of inconsistent parenting can lead to mood disorders, personality disorders (even schizophrenia) and substance abuse in adult life. In my experience, disorganized attachment creates a terrible paradox in adult life: you have such an overwhelming fear of being rejected that you reject everyone in a failed attempt to protect yourself from rejection. As a result, you live in a state of confusion and despair; you continually sabotage relationships to prove your own underlying belief that people will let you down. It's a vicious circle. (See positive feedback loops, in Chapter 9, 'Comfortably numb'.)

The signs of disorganized attachment are:

- a pathological fear of rejection
- an inability to regulate emotions
- contradictory behaviours
- high levels of anxiety
- distrusting others
- exhibiting signs of other attachment styles, such as avoidant and anxious.

If you experienced disorganized attachment as a child, it will have affected you deeply. Your behaviour will be unpredictable and at times very destructive. You can move between being distant and independent, and being clingy and very emotional. This is the ter-rible paradox that drives you – you desperately seek love yet push partners away because you also fear love. Interestingly, this fear of love doesn't make you stop seeking love but, rather, causes you to seek it out, then reject it once you find it. This constant state of flux between security and fear can plunge your life into chaos.

I have often found that people who experienced this type of

attachment never gained any solid sense of themselves as a child. They often speak of not feeling grounded, or not having any principles, of lacking that guiding light. At times, they feel like they are bobbing around in the ocean, with no horizon in sight. This lack of a sense of self adds further to their erratic behaviour.

You are not a prisoner

The four attachment styles range from healthy and loving to insecure and deeply unsettling, but the important thing to know is that you are not a prisoner of your attachment style and the behaviour it has fostered in you.

Learning about these styles, and figuring out your style, allows you to understand how you interact with your loved ones and why you react in certain ways. This awareness can heal the most dysfunctional childhood experience of attachment.

I'll give you an example of doing this in practice.

—

CASE STUDY
Building trust

I had a client who really distrusted her youngest child. She found him sneaky and unlikeable. As we went through her life story and compiled her genogram, it became immediately obvious what was coming up for this mother.

She had been raised in a distant, nuclear family and experienced an anxious attachment type, and as a result communication was incredibly problematic for her. She felt threatened by her child's expressions of emotion, and she came to realize that this was sparked by the inconsistent messages around emotions that she had received as a child. Once she started understanding her own childhood experience, she was able to focus on building trust with her son.

She had to intentionally make the effort to think beyond her first, emotional instincts and work on trusting him and seeing him as trustworthy. When she did this, the tension in her life decreased considerably.

—

What you can do

First, identify which of the attachment styles was the one you experienced as a child. Can you see it in your adult behaviour? Do you feel that those childhood experiences are colouring your beliefs and behaviour?

Look at the attributes of secure attachment again – is there one you would particularly like to cultivate in your own life? Over a two-week period, focus on introducing that aspect into your daily life. It will mean going against your knee-jerk reactions and will force you to think before reacting.

Let's say you have an anxious attachment style and you realize you shape-shift to suit other people. Over the course of the next two weeks, start to be more authentic. Say no when you don't want to do something. Be more honest about how you are feeling. See if this changes how you talk to yourself.

YOUR GENOGRAM

Let's get your genogram under way.

1. On a sheet of paper, write down your grandparents' names, dates of birth and death, and any relevant medical information. Use the symbols shown earlier to indicate the nature of their relationship.
2. Draw in their children and connect them to their spouses – just as in a normal family tree. Again, indicate the type of relationship between each couple.
3. From your parents, draw lines down to show you and your siblings. You can add in biographical information as well, if you wish.
4. To the basic picture, write in the attachment style you had with your primary caregiver in early development. Do the same, as best you can, for your siblings.

5. Make a list of the possible adverse effects of that attachment style on your adult life and relationships. Do you believe this is impacting your life currently? How? What could you do to stop this attachment style from impacting your life?

3. How we learn – welcome to your brain!

Here's a moment from my early childhood that I stored in my memory: when I was about three years old, my parents had a house party to celebrate the fact that my father was leaving RTÉ to start a new job in Cork, writing for the *Irish Times*. Unbeknownst to them, one of the guests had brought poitín in a 7up bottle.

I don't remember getting up the next morning, I don't remember getting dressed or what I was wearing. I don't even remember what I was feeling or thinking as I came downstairs, but where my memory does come online is taking a swig from the 7up bottle. I can still recall the horror as it burnt my oesophagus. The taste was totally incongruent – unlike anything I had experienced before. I dropped the bottle and ran away from it, crying hysterically. For months afterwards, whenever I saw a 7up bottle I would start to cry. In fact, it took a few years before I ventured to taste 7up again. My parents' reassurance and my brothers' carefree guzzling of it failed to convince me that it was safe to drink. I eventually did try it again, but tentatively, taking a tiny sip, calibrating the danger, then finally accepting it was okay to drink. But to this day, when I see a 7up bottle, that memory immediately comes to mind.

Many things come up for me about that moment – the carelessness of leaving a 7up bottle with poitín around the house, my parents' shame when they realized what had happened – but also, more importantly, how memories become coded and recalled throughout life.

As you read this, some of what you are processing is getting sorted, coded and stored, filed away so it is available to be revisited later in your life. Sometime in the future, be it a month, a year, or decades from now, something will happen that will trigger a recollection of something I said in this chapter, and you will think, *Oh, that's what he meant*. We often experience something in a moment, but we might not realize the impact it has had on our lives for a long time. It gets stored away, to be replayed in the future. Sometimes our subconscious persistently shows us something we don't fully understand – a memory, a thought, an idea. When this happens, it usually means we are attempting to process something significant that we have embedded into our coded memory for a reason.

Memories are not simply thoughts – they can directly impact our feelings and emotions in the present. For example, we have all become flushed with embarrassment, remembering something we wished we hadn't said or done. The body is reacting physiologically to a memory.

The function of memory

The human brain is designed to protect us and to make us reproduce. That's it really. All the other stuff we do is a consequence of the complicated world we have created. But, at base, it is all about those two primary functions: survival and reproduction. Our evolution didn't have to prioritize memory, except for the fact that it keeps us safe. If one of our tribe was eaten by a predatory animal and we forgot that experience, we wouldn't have lasted long as a species. Memory is vitally important for our survival. You put your hand on a hot saucepan and it burns your skin. You certainly do not analyse that pain. There's no point engaging the neocortex for sophisticated analysis: *My! That is quite hot. I don't think I've ever touched something so hot. Oh, actually I do remember now, in 1986 I put my hand into the fire to retrieve my favourite blazer, yes, I think that might well have been hotter.* That type of analysis would ensure your hand melted down to the bone by the time you removed it. Your hand reacts without you even consciously thinking about the pain. That comes afterwards, as you analyse what happened to make your hand react like that – and you file away a clear memory of the moment so as not to reproduce it.

The neocortex is vital for higher order thinking, but we also need a short cut – a system that makes us react instinctively – and that system is provided by the amygdala. It receives information on a straight pathway from our senses, which is crucial when we experience something in our environment that threatens us. Professor

Jeffrey Gray argues that the amygdala plays a far more important role in human behaviour than simple fight-or-flight responses. Based on animal studies, Gray has concluded that damage to the amygdala produces a much wider range of emotional deficits than would be expected if it were a purely defensive structure. He points to the example of monkeys with damaged amygdalae who were no longer fearful of humans. The monkeys' coded memory of humans had been rewritten and therefore was not anxiety-provoking. In fact, wider scientific research suggests that the amygdala plays a significant role in the functioning of memory, as well as in the modulation of social and emotional behaviour.

One of the most fascinating documentaries I have watched in recent years is *Free Solo*. It captures Alex Honnold's 2017 attempt to climb, without ropes, the sheer face of El Capitan in Yosemite National Park. It is a remarkable documentary, but also a difficult watch for anyone with a functioning amygdala. The grave peril in which Honnold places himself when climbing this magnificent granite rock formation is contrasted with his serene and calm demeanour. At times, I was watching it through my fingers. As I did, I was thinking, *This guy must have damaged his amygdala as a kid, or some genetic disease impacted its development.* Interestingly, Honnold did undergo a fMRI scan, to see the inner workings of his brain. What the scan revealed was that his amygdala was intact but did not respond to external stimuli – it was inactive when presented with stressful stimuli.

The reason I am mentioning the amygdala and anxiety is because memory plays such an important role in our daily lives: in how we perceive, react to and navigate the world. And where do we receive most of our memories from? Our family of origin, of course, that vast repository of first experiences and role-modelling. Home is where the start is, which means that everything you know and believe is rooted in all the information and feedback that built the cortical columns in your brain in your early, formative years. Those columns are the storage depot of all your unique experiences and knowledge. When you entered the world after birth, your brain embraced every single thing it saw and felt. Each of those unique experiences added up to create your unique interpretation of the world – your personal world view.

I have three children myself, and observing them as they grow gives such incredible insights into human behaviour. They have had similar experiences, the same holidays, for the most part the same parenting approach, and yet each of them experiences and processes the world in their own unique way. What one child holds as a significant memory is quickly forgotten by another. The brain does not process and interpret information in a standard manner across all human beings – far from it!

Filtering and sorting

Memory is paramount to how we experience our present life. Our brain often stores a memory whole. For example, when you see a bicycle, you don't really see the pedals, brakes and saddle – well, you do see them, but you see it as a whole. You don't think, *Oh, look at the saddle, the pedals, the wheels* . . . You simply think, *Bike*. But if you saw wheel spokes burning in a bonfire, without any other evidence available, your brain would still 'see' the whole and think, *Bike*. Your brain would fill in the gaps, based on previous experience, allowing you to interpret your present experience.

Our brain remembers by filtering parts into a whole, and vice versa. Before the brain stores information, it uses attention filters that rapidly decide the level of importance to attach to the observed information. We cannot store and recall every single thing we witness in any given day. As you read this, for example, your brain is focused on the words on the page, while your environment is being filtered out – probably only coming into view now because I have mentioned it. We simply could not process every single bit of information we encounter during our day. There's just too much. Therefore, the brain has to decide what is significant enough to store into sensory memory, short-term memory and long-term memory.

- *Sensory memory* is a mental representation of how environmental events look, sound, feel, smell and taste.
- *Short-term memory* refers to information processed in a short period of time. It is stored in the lower part of the temporal lobe, which also houses the amygdala.

- *Long-term memory* involves the storage and recall of information over long periods of time, which is stored in the neocortex.

There are two types of long-term memory: explicit memory and implicit memory.

EXPLICIT MEMORY

When you have to intentionally remember something, this information is stored in your explicit memory. We use these memories constantly to navigate daily life. When we think about the time at which we are due to meet a friend, or recall a phone number, this is coming from our explicit memory. Anything you must consciously bring into awareness is explicit memory.

IMPLICIT MEMORY

Information that you don't have to purposely try to remember is stored in implicit memory. These are skills you've learned that you don't have to relearn in order to perform them, like whistling, riding a bike, playing an instrument, or typing. You can do these things without thinking about them. You might even catch yourself whistling and think, *I didn't even realize I was whistling*. This is implicit memory.

THE DIFFERENCES BETWEEN EXPLICIT AND IMPLICIT MEMORY

Explicit memory:

- is encoded to memory and later retrieved
- is often formed deliberately through rehearsal
- is often encoded unconsciously and tied to emotions
- may be drawn into conscious awareness through associations.

Implicit memory:

- becomes automatic over time with repetition
- begins with learning skills and mastering a task

- can result in priming (see below), or responding the same way to similar stimuli
- is often dependent upon context and cues.

The physical effects of memory

Once information has been deemed significant enough to be stored in long-term memory, it can be recalled at any moment in the future. This becomes very significant when we experience trauma. Parts of the traumatic experience can become embedded into our memory in such a way that a smell or a sound can provoke the memory, pushing it to the surface of our consciousness. When this happens, it can kickstart a physical reaction, particularly if the memory is threatening or distressing. The brain remembers, the body reacts. This is why we often become anxious without any direct external negative stimulus, because memory can provoke a physiological response in the present. That can be quite frightening to experience. A panic attack can seem to come out of nowhere, but often a memory has triggered it.

One side effect of a very negative childhood is that our internal warning system gets pushed into a hyperactive state. It's always switched on. This means we don't need to encounter any negative stimulus in order to experience the physical symptoms of anxiety. This is what terrifies people. I hear it so often in my clinic: 'I don't know what's happening to me, but out of nowhere I'm anxious, I can't breathe, my heart pounds, and I think I'm going to faint.' This sort of experience can be very upsetting and disruptive.

I had one client tell me: 'I was heading out for the night. I was walking down the street, really looking forward to meeting my friends and having a night out. All of a sudden – whack! – I was struck by panic.' Her last thought was how happy she was, and then she was kneeling on the street, hyperventilating. Now, she was afraid of it happening again. And, of course, fear is anxiety's greatest fuel.

As we delved into what had caused this sudden experience of panic, she recalled a moment from her childhood when she was happy. She was out picking flowers and playing with a friend. Her parents called her to come home. Inside the house, they sat her down and explained they were separating. She described feeling faint, weak and unable to breathe in that childhood moment. She was about eight years old. This event had become embedded into her long-term memory, which meant it could be activated at any time. Walking past the flowers in St Stephen's Green and feeling happy had brought up that moment. There she was, walking down the street, about to meet her friends, but in reality she was walking into an unprocessed traumatic childhood memory. For her, it didn't feel like an act of remembering. It felt like being ambushed and attacked by a memory – that's a horribly out-of-control feeling to experience. It was no wonder it left her feeling fearful.

This is what happens when you have negative childhood experiences stored in your implicit memory. Those memories can be activated at any time, by any external association to that memory. That's why, when your body reacts to the memory, it can seem like it came from nowhere. That can be very frightening, because you feel like you have lost control of yourself. The more you feel like that, the more rigid you become, and now your entire warning system is on alert.

—

CASE STUDY
Panic response

I had a client who came to me because she was experiencing panic attacks. It happened every time she got close to her workplace: she became overwhelmed with fear, her heart rate increased, she felt nauseous, she couldn't think clearly, and she felt faint. She was totally stumped by this recent development in her life. She didn't hate her job, had been enjoying it up until this sense of panic came into her life. In her perception, this had come out of nowhere, and it was making her life unbearable.

In our conversations it became clear that she had grown up in a highly conflicted family. Her father was an aggressive man, prone to fits of rage. She recalled hiding in her closet while her father smashed plates, screamed and hit her mother. As she recalled this memory, she became overwhelmed. She started to experience all those feelings that were overwhelming her as she approached her workplace. In her memory of that moment, she was powerless, vulnerable and weak. Her father was a powerful man who exerted incredible authority over her as a child. And now, this memory was disrupting her adult life.

As we explored her working life, she explained that a new manager had taken over and she found him difficult to work with. He was 'boorish'. One evening, I asked if I could walk with her to her workplace; it wasn't far from my clinic. We headed off, and as we got closer, I asked her, 'Do you feel anything?' She didn't. As we climbed the stairs to her office, I asked again, 'Anything now?' She was visibly disappointed that there were no signs of anxiety.

As we walked back to my clinic, she apologized for wasting my time. Her conclusion was that she must have felt safe in my presence. She wasn't wrong in her analysis. Her alert system was being provoked to fire by this new 'boorish' boss. She had an image of herself as that vulnerable girl, hiding in the closet, terrified of being found. This was a very potent image in her mind.

Yet, it was only when I interviewed that 'child in the closet' that we had a real breakthrough. In that conversation, she revealed that being weak had protected her. Her father didn't pick on her because he viewed her as vulnerable and weak. She declared in the therapy room one day, 'I'm not that vulnerable girl any more. I don't think I ever was. I just learned how to survive that man.' Through tears, she realized her strength. I explained to her that she was no longer that child in the closet. We had to work to tear down that memory of her hiding, and replace it with a new thought: how competent and resilient she was to have survived such a difficult childhood. It was only when she started to view herself as powerful, and no longer that frightened child, that the sense of panic began to ebb away.

It provides a good illustration of the fact that how we interpret our early childhood memories is vitally important for our progress as adults. If we change the significance of the memory, we can change the impact it has on our current life.

—

The dangers of priming

Priming is an important feature of implicit memory. Research suggests that when we are having a conversation with someone, we do not hear what they are saying by analysing the frequencies of the sounds that enter our ears and then determining the words that those frequencies form. Instead, we utilize what is known as 'top-down processing'. Our brains first recognize speech sounds, then use context cues to interpret the meaning of those speech sounds. This is a fascinating insight and explains why we often completely misinterpret each other.

Context cues are taken from our lived experience, from what we know. This means that when we are listening to someone talking, we are filtering out unfamiliar content. In other words, we are primed to hear what we are expecting to hear.

Here is a story to illustrate this. When The Beatles first met Bob Dylan, he was surprised they had never smoked marijuana because he had heard them singing 'I get high, I get high' in their hit song 'I Want To Hold Your Hand'. John Lennon explained to Dylan that the line was, in fact, about wanting to hide. Why, Dylan wondered, would anyone want to hide the fact they loved someone?

This exchange reveals something about how we hear and listen. When the sound we hear is ambiguous, our brain fills in the missing information as best it can. Dylan was no stranger to getting high in those early days, so when he was confronted with the ambiguous sounds of Lennon's vocals, he translated the meaning within the context of what he knew, and to him it had to be, 'I get high.'

I regularly experience the same phenomenon when working with couples who are in a long-term relationship. They frequently use short cuts in conversations by predicting what the other is going to say, and whatever is actually said becomes irrelevant. I often allow the conversation to continue, making notes of direct quotes from each partner. At the end, I ask them what they heard, and generally it is an incredibly negative interpretation. When I read back the quotes, it is a striking moment. They have to confront the fact that they are not listening to each other's words, but instead are anticipating what each other will say. Couples in conflict are primed to hear negative talk from their partner.

Instant negativity? Come in, I was expecting you

Many studies have found that people who are experiencing depressed mood are more likely to show implicit recall of negative information. People who are not depressed are more likely to implicitly recall positive information. This means that those who are depressed are primed to *recall* negative memories. If you couple that with being primed to *hear* negativity, a person can quickly become enveloped by pessimistic thinking.

As you read this book, your brain is going through a series of complicated computations. Your fingers are touching the paper, and that touch has triggered a retrieval cue. Your brain is processing the touch and bringing memory into play, to tell you that it is familiar and that you have experienced it in the past and it isn't a threat. Your system is therefore calm. Now, imagine as you flicked through the pages that one of them was randomly scorching hot. You would drop the book instantly, without thinking. The coded memory that you previously held about the touch of paper would get rewritten. Next time you encountered a piece of paper, you wouldn't be as carefree as you were before the negative experience. More than likely, you would move away from the paper, viewing it as a threat. The memory of the scorching-hot paper incident would be replayed by your brain to protect you from harm.

Recent research by neuroscientist Jeff Hawkins suggests that rather than touch triggering retrieval cues, what actually happens is that all of our experiences are embedded in the billions of cortical columns in the brain (where memory is stored) and therefore we are predicting experience before it occurs. Think for a moment: before you touched the paper of this book, did you know what it was going to feel like? When you prepare to put your key in the front door lock, do you already anticipate the metallic sound of the key hitting the grooves before you do it? When you put your hand into your pocket, do you know what that is going to feel like before you do it?

Hawkins' research suggests that we do know. This is hugely significant in terms of the role memory plays in our interactions with the world around us. If we store memory of the world so that we can predict what experiences are going to be like, what happens when we have experienced regular negativity in our family of origin? How does that impact the way we experience the world as adults? This brings us back to perception, and to the negative recall evident in people who are depressed: if we are always predicting negative experiences, that is exactly what we will experience. If the negative experiences are top of the pile, first to hand, they will seep into every interaction and impact our levels of joy and happiness.

We all become fearful at times; that is necessary for our survival. But it's how you manage that, and how you speak to yourself about who you are, that makes the difference. A number of years ago, I carried out a piece of research for a book I was writing, *Parenting the Screenager*. I wanted to find out what made one child resilient and another child fearful, anxious and unable to meet the demands placed on them. What I noticed very early on in my research was that children who were resilient were able to see adversity as temporary, whereas children who were not resilient spoke about challenges and adversity in concrete, immovable terms: 'Things will never get better', 'I'll always be the same', 'I'll never be able to deal with that.' A resilient child spoke in much more hopeful terms: 'It won't always be like this', 'It will pass', 'I was fine yesterday, I'll be fine tomorrow.' Their ability to reframe adversity was remarkably more refined than a child who was struggling with resilience.

That teaches us an important lesson: perception is everything. How you process and interpret the information you are experiencing will determine positive or negative perception. And how was your perception of the world formed? It was created by the behaviours modelled by your parents, by the vast and complicated experiences you encountered, and processed, in your formative childhood years.

For this reason, it is essential that we are aware of the negative memories living inside us. We can't get rid of memories that we have coded, even if we would very much like to. If we try to ignore or block them, it will prove self-defeating. Our memories are always there, motivating us and driving us forward, or holding us back. We must learn to interpret those memories so that they no longer wield power in our present lives, no longer make us fearful and prevent us from thriving.

The way forward is to change the context of those memories, so the story we tell ourselves about who we are becomes more positive. We can change our perception, we can reframe the story, we can be aware and ready when the negativity tries to crowd in. By becoming aware of the memories, we can lessen and contain their hold over us.

What you can do

If you have discovered some parts, or even the whole, of a particularly troubling event in your childhood, it is important that you realize that these events have no actual power in your present life. Writing that out and reading it to yourself is an important first step towards debunking those early paradigms you established about yourself.

Paradigms are the beliefs or stories you have come to tell yourself about who you are, for example, 'I'm weak', 'I'm lazy', 'I'm not valuable', 'People don't like me.' They are old ideas that drive your current behaviour. By writing them down, you can hear how you speak to yourself.

When I do this with clients, I read their words back to them and ask, 'Would you call me those things?' They immediately protest that they wouldn't. I point out that they have more compassion for a stranger than for themselves.

Once we start to hear how we talk to ourselves, it's much harder to berate ourselves unconsciously.

YOUR GENOGRAM

1. Think about your key childhood memories. Write down some you think were difficult to experience.

2. How do you think you stored that experience into memory – as a whole experience, or in parts? If you think there might be some associated objects connected to that memory, what might those be? Write them out and ask yourself, do those objects trigger a negative memory for you?

3. Think about your recall. Do you think you are primed for negative or positive memories?

PART THREE

The Making of You – Understanding Your Family

I WAS THE YOUNGEST OF THREE BROTHERS. THE FEELING OF being the last family member, that you have to fight to be heard and taken into account, is a unique youngest child experience. The eldest is the only child to experience living alone with their parents, until another child arrives on the scene and disrupts all that single focus. That can be a very tricky moment for the eldest child to experience. They can struggle to compromise, having always had things their own way. They can also have an incredible amount of responsibility placed on their shoulders, which they might later come to resent. The middle child can get caught between two big personalities and often become self-contained and selfless, putting the needs of the youngest before their own.

The position in which you arrived into your family was outside your control, but there are invisible rules dictating those dynamics that can cause tension and conflict. I was the youngest, and personality-wise I was open and extraverted. I never realized that I could be a bit overpowering, that I could dominate a room, you'd certainly know I was there. Being the youngest is almost like getting to traverse a thick jungle with ease; the brothers ahead have machete'd the thick undergrowth, leaving the way free for you to pass. That can breed resentment from the older siblings, as they see you gliding along, carefree, and not appreciating all they had to endure so you could move with such freedom. That can be an unspoken resentment that lingers long after childhood has ended. Often the families I meet in my clinic are coming for help because those old patterns and dynamics are still playing out in adulthood.

Growing up, I felt like I had been dropped into the wrong family. I didn't have much in common with my brothers; I loved them, I was close to my middle brother, but I never felt like we shared the same view of the world. They never really caused my parents too much trouble. Maybe they were just better at messing than I was. I had been in some trouble in primary school. I found school in those early days held nothing of interest for me. I'd spend most of my days looking out the old prefab window, dreaming about an exciting life out there, waiting for me. I couldn't stand the sight or smell of chalk; the sound it made on the blackboard caused me to literally shudder. Irish classes, with their slide shows of children kicking a football, numbed my soul. I struggled to understand what any of school had to do with who I was or wanted to be.

Some days, I didn't go to school. I'd get the bus into town and just walk around. Other days, I'd go to the cinema or go to the amusements with a friend of mine. I didn't really feel connected to anything in those days. I loved sports and played everything. But I didn't feel that school was something that could offer me anything of worth. It was something you had to endure, certainly not enjoy. I also think coming last in my family, with two academic brothers ahead of me, kind of made me feel like I had no place. The academic role was gone, the good intelligent son was already taken, so what the hell could I be?

I often meet this same feeling in my clinic. I am so aware of the sadness in the room as a teenager describes his brother or sister as 'the brainy one'. I hear the same despondent sentence: 'I'm not book smart like my brother/sister.' They believe their parents respect their sibling more because they are 'the clever one'. Comparison is a thief of human joy. It's utterly unique to us as a species, and it causes terrible suffering. Who is the first person you start comparing yourself to? Naturally, it's your siblings. That's why sibling rivalry is so intense – and can last a lifetime.

4. Family dynamics

In sociological terms, there are five main family types. The usual approach is to separate extended families from blended families, but I will include them all here together, because blended families have become far more prominent in recent times. Learning about your family type, and developing an understanding of how it affects your life, can bring a strong sense of clarity, particularly if you are struggling with family dynamics, or attempting to change particular problematic interactions or personal behaviours.

The five family types are:

- nuclear family
- single-parent family
- blended family
- same-sex family
- grandparent family.

Nuclear family

The nuclear family generally comprises two parents (usually married or in a common-law relationship), with one or more children who are either biological or adopted. The two parents raise their children together in the family home as a single unit.

Research shows that any stable two-parent household, regardless of the parents' genders, can create a healthy, loving environment for their children to thrive. The traditional view of the nuclear family, described by the social anthropologist Bronislaw Malinowski in the early 1900s, referred to two people of the opposite sex who are married and have a child or children together. However, the modern definition of a nuclear family now includes same-sex marriages. The research clearly shows that children who grow up in a stable home with two loving parents have a higher chance of upward economic mobility when compared with children who grow up in unstable home environments without two parents.

The strengths of a healthy nuclear family include:

- generally more financially stable
- children are raised within a stable parenting unit
- the values and principles of parents are passed on to children
- emphasis on health and education
- can provide emotional, financial and spiritual support
- consistency and structure allow children to thrive
- focus on good communication
- connection to family during ageing.

The weaknesses of an unhealthy nuclear family include:

- exclusion of the extended family of one parent can lead to isolation and stress
- pressure placed on one member (generally the mother) can cause burnout and resentment
- can struggle with alternative views, meaning conflict resolution becomes hindered
- can become too child-focused, resulting in self-centred children who have a narrow view of the world
- children can develop an unrealistic expectation that the world will revolve around them
- parents can be overly involved in the children's world, solving all their issues, which depletes children's ability to manage and cope with normal ups and downs
- small support system.

It is important to note that healthy families are not always ideal or perfect. They may possess some of the characteristics of dysfunctional families, but not all the time.

Some of the main causes of dysfunction in families include:

- addiction
- abusive parent
- strict, controlling parents
- permissive parents
- mental health of parent
- the impact of serious/tragic family events.

The nuclear family can be dysfunctional in various ways at various times. The key types of dysfunction give rise to different issues in adulthood.

Chronic conflict family

This type of family communicates in a harmful way: conflict is heightened and dangerous and often leaves wounds festering. Neuroscience tells us that prolonged exposure to this type of family can damage a child's neurochemistry, causing increased levels of stress and feelings of insecurity. The child's attachment with its caregiver becomes ruptured. This can lead to an adult who is quite duplicitous because they have learned in childhood to hide who they are or to avoid conflict at all costs because it wasn't safe.

Pathological household

This is where one or more caregiver is living with a severe psychological or mental health disorder or impairment due to addiction. This generally causes the household to run an inverted hierarchy, with the children forced to take on the parenting role. Children who experience this type of family are far more likely to develop mental health issues in adult life.

Chaotic household

This is an environment that is poorly organized due to parents' lack of competence, lack of time, et cetera. There are no visible boundaries, rules or expectations placed on the children. Attachments are often very insecure as parents are inconsistent in their parenting approach. Older siblings often take on the role of caregiver, and may leave home early to escape the chaos. Children who have to cope with this environment can often become quite obsessive as they desperately search for order to ward off the chaos. This can motivate them to become almost pathologically rigid and controlling. Everything they do must be perfect. There is no room for uncertainty or clutter. Ironically, this search for order eventually collapses in adulthood and plunges their life into chaos. They lose control by attempting to control everything.

Dominant-submissive household

This is a household that is run by an autocratic parent who rules over the family like they are the tsar of a small country. Generally, all family members are unhappy and unable to express who they are. However, they tend to be passively obedient to the dominant figure in order to prevent conflict from breaking out. Children can rebel against this type of family by leaving early.

Emotionally distant families

The parents have usually experienced attachment issues during their own childhood and find it difficult to express love to their own children. The children learn to repress their feelings too, and this often leads to them being uncomfortable with intimacy in adult life.

Single-parent family

The numbers of single-parent families have been rising steadily since the 1960s. The single parent likely never married or is separated, widowed or divorced. Sociologists point to a multitude of factors that have led to the increase in single-parent families, such as the relaxation of gender roles, a much more positive attitude towards independence, and a sense of confidence in being able to achieve positive parental goals regardless of having a spouse or not.

I have worked with many single-parent families over the years and, in terms of difficulties, enmeshment has generally been the most prominent issue. Many families admit that their identities have become entangled and stuck, often causing a failure to thrive for all family members. The parent doesn't forge friendships, or a new relationship, because the child becomes their world; the child becomes the parent's confidant and ally, and therefore doesn't have time for other friends. This can force the child to grow up quickly, but it can also deplete their sense of hope for the future; they are caught listening to the adult world's perspective on life and relationships. I had a mother tell me recently, 'I guess I knew we were dug into each other, which wasn't good for either of us, but I just didn't know how to dig us out.'

In my experience, the impact on boys and girls of a dysfunctional single-parent family differs. Boys tend to act out, and research shows they are more likely to be diagnosed with ADHD. In single-parent families where the father is not present, girls tend to internalize their struggles with his absence, and the impact is more often represented in the relationships they form as adults. They struggle to trust people and often seek out similar partners; they replicate their childhood experience by entering into relationships that are doomed to fail.

Research shows that girls appear to be more resilient in the face of family instability and stress than boys.

The strengths of a healthy single-parent family include:

- family members can become very close. The wider family can rally around and support the single parent, providing the child with emotional and financial support
- the parent and child can develop a very close relationship as they work together to make the family function
- develops a child's resilience and teaches self-sufficiency
- positive parenting approaches. Rather than relying on gender-specific roles, single parents tend to choose positive parenting over punitive, authoritarian parenting styles
- less opportunity for conflict in the house.

The weaknesses of an unhealthy single-parent family include:

- financial burden on the family system relying on one income
- the pressure on the parent to work full-time and afford childcare can be immense
- parent burnout more likely
- parent can feel lonely as they attempt to single-handedly meet the demands of their child
- enmeshment. Child and parent identities can become fused, which can cause problems in adolescence when the child attempts to assert their own identity
- child receives only one perspective, which might result in a narrow world view.

Blended family

A blended family is one where people who have children from a previous relationship start a new relationship and raise those children together as a new family unit. They might also have children together and add these into the family, creating a new dynamic.

Blended families are far more common today than ever before. Three out of four people who go through a divorce will marry again, and close to half of all marriages today are at least second marriages for one partner (according to the Pew Research Center). Recent data confirm that about 16 per cent of children live in blended families. Blended families are more popular than ever, and increasing numbers of children are being raised this way.

The strengths of a healthy blended family include:

- single parents often struggle financially, whereas blended families can ease the financial strain
- parents can become happier due to the new relationship and support
- wider perspective for children, which can decrease enmeshment

- children can develop resilience as they learn to manage the changing family dynamic
- children have a wider family network.

The weaknesses of an unhealthy blended family include:

- sibling rivalry with non-biological children can be especially bitter
- the child can suffer from identity confusion as they try to understand who they are in this new family dynamic
- mixed feelings about step-parent can cause conflict, for example, if the child resents the adult who is taking their parent away from them, as they see it
- children can fight for parental attention
- financial difficulties can occur if the family is quite large and there are many needs to meet
- previous strong bonds between parent and child can become weakened in this more complicated dynamic
- new family routine can be difficult for the child to adjust to.

Same-sex family

The legalization of same-sex marriage in many countries in 2015, and the increasing social acceptance of LGBTQI+ rights, means that families headed by same-sex parents are far more commonplace today than ever before. The children of the relationship are either adopted or biologically related to one parent.

Same-sex families are really just modern nuclear families – two parents raising their children together in a single family unit. The research highlights that what really impacts a child's development is not the gender of their parents but the quality of the relationship with those parents or caregivers.

The strengths of a healthy same-sex family include:

- children develop broader and more tolerant views of the world

- they are secure as both parents provide a loving environment for the child
- financial security
- same-sex parents intentionally enter into parenthood after much consideration
- stable home environment.

The weaknesses of an unhealthy same-sex family include:

- children can be targeted and bullied
- potentially limited view of gender as children will see relational dynamics through one gender only.

Grandparent family

A grandparent family is when one or more grandparents raise their grandchild (or grandchildren). This type of family is also becoming more commonplace. In my experience, this family emerges when the primary caregiver is unable to meet the needs of the child due to financial pressure or substance abuse, or there is a new step-parent and they do not get along with the child. In some cases, the child chooses to live with their grandparent because they have a stronger bond with them.

The strengths of a healthy grandparent family include:

- grandparents and grandchildren form a close bond
- keeps children from feeling hopeless and alone
- prevents children from running away or entering foster care.

The weaknesses of an unhealthy grandparent family include:

- income could be an issue as grandparents may not be working
- their health may not be suitable to meet the demands of an active grandchild

- can cause strain and conflict with their own child
- may struggle to understand the needs of a modern child.

The lasting effect of family dynamics

The family you came up in presented you with a unique set of challenges. How you learned to manage the childhood you had to navigate has affected you deeply.

Think of an issue in your life currently. How should you go about solving that problem? Maybe in the past you avoided the issue, because that was a strategy you used in childhood and it worked to some degree. Maybe you obsessively think about it but don't act, because you doubt yourself and are very critical of your ability to make the right decision. You wait for others to make the decision for you – at least that way, you don't have to take responsibility for the decision when it inevitably doesn't work out. Maybe you like to control every aspect of the issue, much to your partner's annoyance or your children's frustrations. Maybe you make the issue worse by impulsively responding to the situation, giving little thought to the consequences of your actions.

Can you spot which type of family each of these behavioural patterns stems from? Can you see the attachment issues running underneath each approach? Make a list of these potential solutions and then try to align the family type and the attachment issue running underneath each intervention. You'll start to see the bigger picture.

Now think about your approach to the issue you are currently dealing with in your own life. What normally drives your response? What are you going to do that is different? Remember, everything in your brain is designed for familiarity, so it will feel awkward and uncomfortable to challenge these old ways of operating. But once you persist, you will notice that you look at problems differently, that you respond differently and, most importantly, that your life isn't as difficult to manage as it once was. This is because you have interrupted old ways of thinking and acting that are unhelpful. We all get stuck from time to time, trying to use the same old interventions to solve current problems. But you can change those old ways. Why do clients leave my clinic feeling empowered and able to face challenges in a new way? It is because they have come to see the problem differently – not through the lens of their expectations, which have been shaped by lived experience, but through the lens of objectivity. They are beginning to view things as they are, not as they expect them to be.

We all have to solve incredibly complex problems during our lives. If the problem-solving tools given to you from childhood are not healthy or helpful, you will continue to use failed solutions when attempting to address your adult problems. Most of us are unaware of the impact of attachment and family type on our every-day lived experience. We think, *Oh that's just me, I'm neurotic about things*. Or, *God, he's so needy, I can never give him enough reassurance*. But the reality is something much deeper and more profound. We believe we are thinking and behaving in new ways, but in reality we did that particular thinking long ago and now we are just rerunning an old, outdated neural circuit loop. We keep thinking and behaving in the same old way, while expecting new and different outcomes.

If you are to thrive, it is necessary to work out how your family is still affecting you, and then to build new ways of thinking about yourself. Only then can you emerge from your childhood and reach your full potential.

What you can do

List some patterns of your behaviour that you know are not good for you.

List patterns of behaviour that you feel would be good for you and that you would like to cultivate. What gets in the way of you living those preferred behaviours?

Work on removing the behaviours that are negative – once you have identified them, this will be much easier. Pay attention to your reactions, and when you see those familiar old behaviours, notice that it's happening and give yourself time to think and then act.

Now that you have identified the behaviours you feel

would be helpful to you, make the effort to intentionally live these behaviours. It will be hard at the start, but it will become natural and more instinctive through repetition – and through seeing positive outcomes as a result of those behaviours.

YOUR GENOGRAM

1. On your genogram, write in your family type.
2. Consider the strengths and weaknesses of your family type in light of what you've discovered in this chapter.
3. Make a list of the positive and negative effects that your family type has had on your development.

5.   *Your position in the family*

Youngest

Generally, if you are the youngest, you might have been described as carefree, easy-going, babyish, wild. Your siblings might describe you as 'always getting what you want', which of course drives you mad because you feel they never take you seriously. In your eyes, you never got what you wanted, which is to be respected like the rest. Parents can often overly coddle the youngest because they realize it's the last time they will have a baby in the house. This can breed resentment from the other siblings, which can be exacerbated in the teenage years when parents, now older and wiser, become more relaxed about rules for the youngest. I certainly experienced this as the youngest in my family. My eldest brother got into trouble for having eight-hole Doc Martens; when I hit adolescence five years later, my fourteen-hole oxblood Docs didn't even raise an eyebrow. Such unfairness can be a fertile breeding ground for discontent among siblings, which can spread into adult life.

As they raise their family, parents can become a little softer in their position. If the eldest child is thriving in life, they can relax a little about adhering strictly to the rules. They have someone ahead who has made it through unscathed, so things are working out fine. But this mollycoddling of the youngest can affect the child's maturity. In my experience, the youngest can really struggle with what is known as 'failure to launch'. Parents might not want the youngest to leave the nest because they are afraid of the changes that will bring.

—

CASE STUDY
Agency is power

I had a mother bring her twenty-eight-year-old son to see me because he was depressed. She felt he was gaming too much. He spent most of his time up in his bedroom.

As the conversation unfolded, it became clear the young man was paralysed by inaction. Everything in his life was done for him. His mother still made him sandwiches going to work, his clothes were washed, dinner was ready for him when he got home. His mother woke him up in the morning. He was stuck in adolescence. And his mother was stuck in not wanting to let go of that situation. She told me that she had a fear of the house without the children.

Developing agency is an essential attribute in life. Without it, we fail to thrive as young adults. Agency is the belief that you have power to make things happen in your life. How you are parented can increase or decrease your sense of agency.

—

The forgotten middle child

If you are the middle child, you might be described as being in the optimal place in the family, between an older sibling who struggled when you arrived and the carefree, infantilized youngest struggling to find their agency. However, your reality might be something else. You might experience the feeling of being forgotten, perhaps caught between the two big personalities of the oldest and the youngest. The middle child can often exhibit high levels of competitiveness as they feel they have to fight and manoeuvre to garner any parental attention. This can provoke the wrath of parents and can earn the middle child the label of 'difficult' or 'needy'.

The middle child can often feel lost in a nowhere land – not old enough to be given responsibility but not young enough to be coddled. Some middle children rebel as a result of this dynamic, while others are mild-mannered and passive. These passive middle children are often dominated by their older siblings; they also understand that the younger child has more needs than they have. As a result, they can spend a lifetime positioned as the peacemaker between the other, more demonstrative siblings.

Some middle children, on the other hand, are very independent and come to rely on themselves early on. They realize – and accept – that their more dominant siblings will always secure parental attention. They are comfortable in their own skin and often leave the family home early.

Eldest

If you are the eldest in the family, it means your parents were very inexperienced when raising you. Nonetheless, it is a privileged status as you were the only child to live with your parents exclusively. Now, that does come with its own pitfalls: you are also the only child who had to share your nest with an interloper. The shock of the arrival of siblings can last a lifetime.

You can easily develop a sense of superiority over your siblings, which can give you a heightened sense of self-righteousness and make you quite bossy. You might also have been given too much responsibility for your siblings' well-being, if your parents leaned on you for support in child-rearing. This can force you into a lifelong role of being reliable and dependable. This, in turn, can cause huge stress, as you feel the pressure to be all things to all people.

Sibling rivalry

I meet many families and conflicted siblings in my work. The issues are generally rooted in early childhood experiences, personality traits, and the position in the family they were thrown into from birth. Your sibling is generally the first person you compare yourself to, and that can be the cause of much suffering. Parents can often unconsciously pit sibling against sibling – subtle comparisons, comments that position one above the other. Parents rarely think their children are listening when they talk about them, but they are, and those comments can be the source of deep-rooted rivalry.

In my clinical experience, siblings often have very fractured relationships and struggle to understand the reason for their conflict. Sibling rivalry is created when children feel one is receiving more attention than the other, or when one is perceived to be endowed with more talents. How you tell your children you love them is very important. Something I say to my own children is, 'I love you the same amount but for different reasons.' This allows children to experience their parents' love without feeling it is a measurable thing. Your sibling relationship is the longest relationship you will ever have with anyone in your life. It is also a very complicated one, especially if you grew up in dysfunction. In my experience, both professionally and personally, when children have grown up in a difficult family environment they often have very strained relationships with each other. In fact, they can often avoid each other's company because it is too painful. They are a reminder of the chaos and dysfunction experienced in childhood. So they avoid each other, which breeds resentment and suspicion.

What I have noticed over the years is that the more conflicted a person is with a sibling, the more likely it is that the sibling reminds them of something they dislike about themselves.

YOUR GENOGRAM

1. Write in your position, and that of each sibling, next to your names on the genogram.
2. Now, make a list of what you think was communicated to you about yourself by your parents and siblings based on your position. Have you lived out those ideas during adulthood?
3. What was communicated about each of your siblings – write those down, too. Looking at this, do

you think the labels assigned to each of you have impacted your sibling relationships?

If you have conflict with a sibling, write down what you think they experienced and how their position impacted them and your relationship with them. Try to see the rupture in your relationship through their eyes. What would they say about the cause of the strained relationship? What would have to change to fix that relationship?

6.   *Personalities at play within the family*

In psychology there are five main personality traits, known as the 'Big Five'. It is important to understand your personality type so you can work on any traits that are holding you back and harness certain traits to improve your life satisfaction.

Understanding your personality type gives you insights into the type of person you are and what you need in order to thrive. For example, an extravert with few friends will suffer massively because they get their energy from being around people and need those connections to feel whole. A person with high levels of neuroticism would be well advised to avoid the uncertain life of an entrepreneur, because the unpredictable ups and downs of that life would be too much to manage.

Those bursting with ideas are generally extraverted and open, but often lack follow-through. They move quickly from one idea to the next and can become disillusioned as they realize their ideas are always just that, ideas. The key thing to understand, though, is that our personality traits are not set in concrete. You can work on them, to decrease or increase them as best fits your needs and your life.

It is very rare to have high levels of more than two or three personality traits. Interestingly, we often marry people who make us the whole person. I have heard many people say over the years about colleagues, 'Why did she marry him? He is incredibly outgoing and she is painfully shy.' We say that opposites attract, but really opposites complement and complete.

We must constantly navigate personality – our own and everyone else's. But we don't always think about that fact. We might find a particular person difficult, we might even really dislike a sibling, but we dismiss it – 'Oh, they're just a difficult person.' But more than likely, someone is in a happy relationship with them – someone might even love them. So, the question we should be asking is, 'What do they see in him / her that I don't see?', 'What is it about my type of personality that jars with their personality?' Again, we must actually think about what their personality is like and then compare it to our own to reach a sound conclusion. This could be one of the most profound insights you gain into a difficult relationship in your life – be it personal or professional. You might be more like the person you dislike than you would care to believe. And what you dislike about them might be something you dislike about yourself. That can be a frightening insight, but ultimately a very helpful one.

As I describe the 'Big Five' here, make a note of the type of personality traits you think you display, then cross-check that with reliable sources. It's often the case that fellow family members are not the most reliable source, because their opinion can be affected by their feelings towards you. You can ask a trusted friend or work colleague, for example, to see if your perception of yourself aligns with the general perception of you.

The 'Big Five' personality traits

You will be adding to your genogram at the end of this chapter, so an understanding of the five personality types will help you to identify more accurately your own personality and that of the significant people in your life. In practice, understanding these key traits will help you to manage yourself and the difficult personalities you encounter.

These traits are:

1. openness
2. conscientiousness
3. extraversion
4. agreeableness
5. neuroticism.

Naturally, we are more complicated than five personality traits, and there are many nuances within each category, but research shows that these five key traits are remarkably universal. Psychologists argue that there is an evolutionary explanation – that these traits represent the most important qualities that shape our social landscape.

We might not think of our personality type shaping our world, but it has more influence than we might realize. An outgoing, open person will experience more in life than someone who believes things never work out. That person will be closed off and not see good or potential around them, while the extravert will expect good things and bounty to come into their life. These two personalities are primed to view the world differently: one will see abundance, one will see only disappointment.

Nature versus nurture

The latest research proposes that personality traits are not dealt out to us by 'nature', and therefore it is not the case that we can never escape them. 'Nurture' – what we observe in the world around us, and how we are treated – plays a huge role in the personality traits we develop.

Whatever our early childhood experiences and family background, we can continue to develop our personality through awareness and effort. We can, for example, improve a trait we feel we might be low in, so that it becomes a strength. That is a liberating thought.

I have met far too many clients who came into my clinic with the self-defeating attitude, 'That's just who I am.' There is nothing more disempowering than the belief, 'That's the way I am, I can't change now.' We can change at any time.

1. Openness

Openness is the ability to be open-minded and imaginative. It includes characteristics such as creativity, imagination and insight. People who are high in openness tend to have a broad range of interests. In my experience, people who are open are generally polymaths – good at many things, and interested in developing themselves by exploring new concepts and ideas.

Open people are curious about the world; they are curious about other people and eager to learn new things and enjoy new experiences.

People who are high in openness:

- are very creative
- are focused on tackling new challenges and enjoy the challenge of something new and different
- are happy to think about abstract concepts
- thrive on uncertainty.

People who are low in openness:

- dislike change
- do not enjoy new things
- resist new ideas
- are not very imaginative
- dislike abstract or theoretical concepts
- like rigid routine and find spontaneity difficult to experience.

People who are high in openness tend to be more adventurous and creative, but they can struggle in a working environment that is restrictive and controlling. In my experience, they struggle in State jobs or rigid bureaucratic roles. In my work in the corporate space, I carry out psychometric tests on professionals. The data reveal very interesting insights into why certain people have been struggling. The answer is glaringly obvious: their personality and the work they do are not a good fit. Often, they are in the wrong working environment for their personality, and it causes huge distress.

What about you? Think about the job you are currently doing. Does your personality type suit the role you are performing? People low in this trait often struggle with abstract thinking and find working environments with vague boundaries challenging.

Think about the family you came from – in what way did your parents use power? Were they authoritarian or were they permissive and had few boundaries? If you are high in openness and your parents were authoritarian, you would have struggled with how rigid your parents were. If you are low in openness and your parents were permissive, this would have caused a significant amount of distress, as your family environment would have been too chaotic to feel secure.

Now put it all together: think about the family you came from, whether you are high or low in openness, and the work you do. Are they all aligned? This is very important because these three aspects have a significant impact on happiness.

2. *Conscientiousness*

Standard features of conscientiousness include high levels of thoughtfulness, good impulse control, and goal-directed behaviours. Highly conscientious people tend to be organized and mindful of details; they plan ahead, think about how their behaviour affects others, and stick to deadlines.

In my experience, people who are high in conscientiousness often try to control every aspect of their lives. Lawyers and accountants, for example, tend to be high in conscientiousness because they have to be – carelessness could be extremely costly. Generally, though, they already have it as a personality trait, so it's a good fit with their choice of career.

The downside is that they can be serious worriers – they worry because they believe this prevents a negative outcome – and this can bring a lot of suffering into their lives. I have met many lawyers and accountants in my clinic, and it's noticeable that control is one of their main responses to negative stimuli. In Chapter 9 ('Comfortably numb') we will look at positive feedback loops in detail, but for now it's enough to know that a feedback loop is anything you do to make yourself feel better in the immediate moment but which, in fact, causes far more problems because it moves you further away from balance in the long term.

It can be a confusing term because the word 'positive' makes it sound like a good thing, but 'positive' means 'rate of growth' in this instance. A quick example of a positive feedback loop in operation is when a person who has a fear of public spaces attempts to go out and break that fear. While standing at the bus stop, they become anxious. When the bus approaches, they feel sick. They can't do it.

They turn and start walking home. Immediately, their panic and anxiety lessen. The moment they are back inside their house, they feel better. But now they are stuck inside. In fact, their life is in a worse place than it was when they were standing at the bus stop. Their anxiety about going outside has increased and will now be more difficult to break. That is a positive feedback loop: you do the thing that makes you feel better right now (going home), but in doing so you are pulling further away from what will actually change things for the better in the long term. These behaviour loops are highly addictive and incredibly destructive.

If a person becomes caught in a feedback loop, when faced with an uncontrollable situation they will fall back on familiar, unhelpful responses, which usually causes their life to spiral into chaos. This is often the source of obsessive thinking, which can become pervasive and spill over into all aspects of life.

—

CASE STUDY
The lawyer with no peace of mind

I had a highly successful lawyer in my clinic explain to me how he couldn't stop worrying. He had just had a baby with his partner and found that while he used to focus his worry on clients and meeting their needs, he was now worrying about the baby. It had become so bad, he couldn't sleep. Worry was stealing any peace he'd once enjoyed. He was even worrying about work he had done twenty years earlier. He feared that what he had done decades ago would come back and bite him in the future. There was no rational basis to his thinking. He was simply looking for reasons to worry.

We traced the origins of his worry back to when he was a child. His family environment was quite chaotic and he had developed worrying as a coping mechanism. His mother used to bring him to mass every day as a child and tell him to pray that something good would happen in their lives. When anything good happened, he believed it was his prayers being answered. This set up a positive feedback loop: if he focused on and prayed about the worry, it would get resolved. This 'worry thinking' had become his way of managing his fears. Now, he was worrying about everything.

Worry was his resting position. He believed that to be without worry would mean his sudden annihilation.

Once we had identified the source of this coping mechanism, he could work on it. But it wasn't about getting him to stop worrying immediately. It was about understanding his personality trait of conscientiousness (and, as we'll see later in this chapter, neuroticism) and his earlier maladaptive response of using worry to soothe his fear of uncertainty. We often become fearful in response to uncertainty, and worry can falsely make us feel like we have some level of control over the unknown future event.

I asked him during one session, 'What would it be like to not worry?'

The pause lasted for minutes. I left it hanging there.

'Jesus, I don't know,' he said finally, 'I've always worried.'

It took time, and there were moments when he still worried excessively. I gave him a phrase that he found very helpful in those moments when he began to fall back into that behaviour: 'Worry doesn't change the outcome of any future event, it only ruins the present.' I also asked him to put aside an hour each evening and to write out all his worry thoughts.

After about two weeks of this, he told me he didn't need to do it any more. He explained, 'It actually seems kind of stupid, sitting there thinking of all my worries.' By introducing him to what he was doing unconsciously, he consciously stopped doing it.

—

Obsessive thinking can be a profoundly debilitating experience. But the biggest mistake a person can make is to attempt to stop thinking those worrying thoughts. If I say to you, 'Don't think of a yellow raincoat. Now, don't think of two yellow raincoats.' What just happened? The more you are fearful of worrying, the more you will worry. You'll end up worrying about worry. We should not try to prevent or suppress worried thoughts, but we do need to see them for what they are, worried *thoughts*, and thoughts are not *facts*, and when we relax about having them, they dissipate.

Your blind spot can only exist until someone points it out to you, at which point it can no longer be a blind spot because you can see it. Once you are aware of your response to negative stimuli, you can no longer respond in an automated, unthinking way. The lawyer who visited me in my clinic had developed the belief that worrying brought about a favourable outcome. Therefore, when he worried about something and it didn't happen, his worrying had fixed the potential negative outcome. It hadn't, of course, but a powerful positive feedback loop had been created. However, the moment he became aware of what he was doing, everything changed.

People who are high in conscientiousness:

- spend time preparing
- finish important tasks right away
- pay attention to detail
- enjoy having a set schedule.

People who are low in conscientiousness:

- dislike structure and schedules
- are untidy and fail to return things
- procrastinate over important tasks
- fail to complete necessary or assigned tasks.

Think about yourself: are you high in conscientiousness? Do you worry a lot? Do you fall into the worry trap? Is your partner a worrier? Do they seek you out for reassurance? When your partner seeks you out for reassurance and you give it, what happens? Have you noticed it doesn't really change their sense of unease? With a person who is high in conscientiousness, it is often the case that the more reassurance you give them, the more they need. This is a mistake parents can make with their children, too. The more you reassure a child, the more the child will come to believe they are incompetent and need reassurance.

Low levels of conscientiousness can get you into all sorts of trouble in the working world. You can be quick to finish a task, without caring about the standard of the work. You can be a very poor planner, and might never achieve a goal because you cannot put a plan in place to successfully go after anything. It can be very frustrating to have low levels of conscientiousness. I often meet children in my clinic who speak about their parents and their lack of planning. The children are annoyed and disappointed as yet another event or holiday turns out to be disastrous. People with low levels of conscientiousness find it difficult to plan and get motivated. They struggle to understand what is required to make something come to life. This can be very difficult to be around, and children suffer when parents lack conscientiousness.

3. Extraversion

People who exhibit extraversion (or extroversion) generally tend to be excitable, sociable, talkative, assertive, enthusiastic (a very important trait for happiness) and have high amounts of emotional expressiveness. People who are high in extraversion are outgoing and tend to gain energy in social situations; being around other people helps them feel energized and excited. Extraverts are highly proficient at creating bonds with people and generally have a large circle of friends. It is no wonder that all the research points to the fact that people with high extraversion are happier than those with high neuroticism (which we will examine later in this chapter). If happiness is rooted in your ability to connect with people, being extraverted significantly increases your chances of being happy.

However, when you are extraverted you can also feel deeply hurt by the criticism of others. People can often be jealous and envious and say hurtful things to bring you down off your happiness pedestal. If you are blindly extraverted, and you believe the words of others, you are susceptible to fluctuating happiness, because it will always be linked to how people speak about you. Being extraverted can mean that you are predisposed to feeling the slights of others more deeply than those who have, say, high levels of conscientiousness.

Understanding *why* people often say negative things about us is very important if we are to be truly happy. People often speak about us negatively, especially when we are doing things that bring attention to us.

CASE STUDY
'Why do they hate me?'

I worked with a teenage girl in my clinic who had aspirations to be a model. She had all the attributes the modelling world looks for: she was a stunning young girl, bright, engaging and very extraverted. But she had been very badly bullied in her school. She couldn't understand what she had done to gain the attention of these girls. Like many people, she questioned what they saw in her that made them hate her so much. They isolated her in school and posted terrible things about her on social media. She was really struggling with her well-being when I met her.

What she had to come to understand is that when you do something that is outstanding or breeds resentment in others, you have to get comfortable with their discomfort. The alternative is to never reach for anything and to keep your head down, but that will not deliver a fulfilling life. And when you look back on your life, you will see that you let the words or ideas of others limit your ideas about yourself. You must never do that. Life is too precious.

As I helped that aspiring young model understand that those girls were to be pitied rather than listened to, I could see the shine come back into her life. Maybe reaching for her dream had provoked their wrath because they lacked the courage to do the same. Maybe it was more about them than about her.

When we gain these insights into the motives of others, it frees us from pain. People can't hurt us with words when we don't believe them. It's when we internalize it and align with it that it really starts to hurt.

People who are low in extraversion (or are introverted) tend to be more reserved and have less energy to expend in social settings. Social events can feel draining, and introverts often require a period of solitude and quiet in order to 'recharge'. Low levels of extraversion can mean you find it hard to make friends. I have met so many clients with low extraversion and nearly all of them find small talk almost impossible. They overthink what they should say, to the point that it sounds awkward and contrived. An extravert rarely thinks about how to make small talk, they just instinctively do it. And, of course, it is something that takes a little practice.

People who are high in extraversion:

- enjoy being the centre of attention
- like to start conversations
- enjoy meeting new people
- have a wide social circle of friends and acquaintances
- find it easy to make new friends
- feel energized when around other people
- say things before thinking about them.

People who are low in extraversion:

- prefer solitude
- feel exhausted by socializing
- find it difficult to start conversations
- dislike making small talk
- carefully think things through before speaking
- dislike being the centre of attention.

4. Agreeableness

Agreeable people exhibit attributes such as trust, altruism, kindness, affection and other pro-social behaviour. People who are high in agreeableness tend to be more cooperative, while those low in this trait tend to be more competitive and sometimes even manipulative.

People who are high in agreeableness:

- have a great deal of interest in other people
- care about others
- feel empathy and concern for other people
- enjoy helping and contributing to the happiness of other people
- assist others who are in need of help.

People who are low in agreeableness:

- take little interest in others
- don't care about how other people feel
- have little interest in other people's problems
- insult and belittle others
- manipulate others to get what they want.

Research suggests that women who are high in agreeableness often suffer as a result of this personality trait. Human babies are born about fifteen months too early. Palaeoanthropology explains that the needs of the baby would exceed the mother's capacity to sustain the pregnancy beyond nine months, which is why the baby is born very early and is very vulnerable. For the species to survive, the primary caregiver must have high levels of agreeableness to ensure the safety of that baby. Science posits this as the reason why women have higher levels of agreeableness than men – because they put the needs of their child before their own.

Society and the expectations it places on women, as well as implicit gender roles, all work to increase a woman's desire to be agreeable as well. This is significant when we think about what can so easily happen to women in life. They find themselves positioned as the 'good daughter', 'good wife', 'good sister', 'good mother'. They can quickly become burnt-out as they take on too much, because too much is expected of them. When our family pins a label like 'the responsible one' or 'the cooperative one' on us, it can super-charge our personality traits.

So, let's just say you are the eldest of three daughters. You have been described as 'the responsible one' and you are agreeable by nature. This is a very common scenario for eldest daughters. You were given the message that to be valued, you must always please others. Your agreeableness is a positive trait, but now it has been appended to this destructive message. Because you are agreeable, you live this out as best you can – and you keep living it out, right into adulthood. As time goes on and this behaviour becomes deeply embedded and therefore feels 'natural', feels part of you, you take on more and more, never questioning it. Eventually, you can end up resenting those you are attempting to please and resenting yourself for not being authentic.

This sort of a bind is very common for people high in agreeableness. When you get caught living like this, you cannot be happy. It is essential that you honestly assess what you are doing, and why, and make the necessary changes for your own well-being.

That is also why agreeable people often marry very disagreeable people. They are attracted to their no-nonsense approach to life. However, as life becomes more complicated, and perhaps children come along, this clash of agreeable versus disagreeable can cause huge conflict. A disagreeable person will be less likely to compromise, because they don't like to agree or bend to suit others. What often happens in this dynamic is the agreeable one does everything and is further positioned as 'the doer', eventually becoming burnt-out or disillusioned with the inequity in the relationship. If this sounds familiar, remember that you teach people how to interact with you. You can change this dynamic by introducing the word 'no' into your lexicon. If you stopped doing everything, what would happen? We often think, *Nobody would do it if I didn't*. Why don't you put it to the test and see what happens? You might be shocked at the result.

5. Neuroticism

Individuals who are high in neuroticism tend to experience mood swings, anxiety, irritability and sadness. Those low in this trait tend to be more stable and emotionally resilient. Neuroticism contributes significantly to harmful life outcomes and affects a person's ability to successfully manage the normal ups and downs of life. A person with high neuroticism responds poorly to environmental stress and can often interpret ordinary situations as threatening or even dangerous. Minor frustrations can escalate to feelings of hopelessness and being overwhelmed.

In my experience, one of the reasons why it is important to be aware if you have high levels of neuroticism is so that this knowledge can inform the type of work you pursue. Someone with high neuroticism would find the entrepreneurial life very challenging; they might be more suited to a job that doesn't require filing tax returns, navigating a fluctuating market space, dealing with employees, and hiring and firing staff. They would be more suited to a job they can easily compartmentalize, so that when they leave work, the job isn't following them home.

People who are high in neuroticism:

- experience a lot of stress
- worry about many different things
- get upset easily
- experience dramatic shifts in mood
- feel anxious
- struggle to bounce back after stressful events.

People who are low in neuroticism:

- are emotionally stable
- deal well with stress
- rarely feel sad or depressed
- don't worry much
- are very relaxed.

—

CASE STUDY
The morbid overthinker

A client came to me because his sleep had become incredibly disturbed on foot of an argument he'd had with a colleague he'd always found difficult. The matter was compounded when he missed a meeting with his boss and this colleague, because he had to collect his sick child from school. The colleague was subsequently put in charge of an account he had expected to be given, and he felt the argument had caused him to slip down the office hierarchy. Office politics are tricky at the best of times, but this easily remedied situation had disrupted his peace considerably and he was ruminating about little else. He couldn't sleep. It was having a massive impact on his sense of well-being.

As we discussed the issue, and how he could approach it in a healthier way, he described how he had been like this since he was a child. He had always overthought every interaction with other people, even the positive ones. As we probed further, it became clear that he had a belief that if he was not worrying, he could be blind-sided by life. He described how he saw the situation: he had let his guard down in the argument with his colleague and now it had 'destroyed everything I have ever worked for'. He went from a single argument to complete career annihilation in one breath.

This type of fatalistic thinking is very common with high-level neuroticism. A neurotic person has a tendency to selectively abstract one event, or feeling, and it becomes representative of the entire experience. They have one bad interaction, or they feel low, and they conclude that everything is terrible in their life.

I advised my client to speak to his boss and discover the exact reason why he hadn't been selected to handle that particular account. He did so. It turned out it had nothing to do with his absence from work to pick up his sick child – in fact, it was to do with his workload. The boss was trying to delegate in a manner that didn't put all the responsibility on his shoulders. The relief he felt as he described that encounter was clear. But all the waste of head space he had given to it!

Another client came to me because he had changed his job and wasn't happy in the new position. He spoke about how he had 'blown up his life', as if everything was in pieces that could never be reassembled. Another client spoke about not achieving a promotion as 'the single most humiliating thing that has ever happened to me'. The hyperbole used by high-level neurotics can have devastating consequences in their lives. Perception is reality. If we think an argument, or not getting a promotion, is devastatingly life-altering, that's what it will become.

—

Growing up with parents who are neurotic can change the chemistry of the brain. Their inability to process stress is handed on to their children. Those children learn to be in a constant state of panic and they use language in a terribly destructive way, like their parents. This means they don't process feelings and events like other children and speak in more absolute terms than children who were raised by open parents.

What you can do

Now that we have looked at the 'Big Five' personality traits and how they can potentially disrupt your life or allow you to thrive, think about the traits you have. Which ones are most dominant in your life? Are they preventing you from thriving? Which traits would you like to have, and what is getting in the way of you developing them?

The more we become aware of ourselves and what motivates our behaviour, the more we can make changes in our lives. Life is not a game of perfect. We don't always get it right, and we often fall back on old negative habits and impulses. When you notice this, don't berate yourself, just pause and change course. Having compassion for yourself is incredibly important. We are often very good at helping others, but not so good at helping ourselves. We wouldn't dare speak to a stranger in the manner in which we speak to ourselves. Listen to that inner critic. Is that voice a tyrant, judging your every move? If so, you need to challenge it, to query it, to stand up to it whenever it tries to bulldoze you. You can work on this and become more positive in your thinking and outlook.

Our parents model personality traits for us that we assimilate in early childhood. Ask yourself which of your parents you are most like. Take out your genogram and write in your parents' key personality traits next to their names, to help you identify this.

Here is an interesting little insight: often the parent we are most like is the parent with whom we have the most conflict. We feel they are harder on us. In my experience, parents often over-parent the child they see themselves reflected in most clearly. They feel they know what that child needs, because they were that child, and so they push them a little harder or hold them accountable a little more than the other kids. As the parent strives to help their child, the child feels the parent is hardest on them. The relationship becomes strained. Often when I draw it out for the parent and child, it is a very poignant moment, as they both see what has been causing the disruption in their relationship.

YOUR GENOGRAM

1. Write in your key personality traits next to your name. Don't fear the answer. Genetic coding is significant in personality, but nurture is paramount. That means your personality is a combination of the two, with nurture playing a bigger role.
2. Write down what personality labels were attached to you and to each sibling within your family. Have you noticed when you go back into your family, for a family gathering, say, that you act out those early descriptions of who you are?
3. Think about those labels. Do you agree with how your family sees you and your personality? Write 'yes' or 'no' to show which ones you dis/agree with.
4. Do you feel your place in your family of origin and your personality traits have had a positive or negative impact on your adult life?
5. Finally, write in the traits you would like to have and be guided by in your life. Now you have identified them, you can work on increasing them.

None of us is static or a finished product. This is great news, because it means we can continue to develop and improve our personality traits. 'Nature' means that certain traits are handed down through the generations, but they are not set in concrete. 'Nurture' allows us to assimilate personality, which means we can all improve and change any traits of our personality. We have agency over them.

PART FOUR

The Child Inside the Adult

WHEN I WAS IN PRIMARY SCHOOL I ACTED OUT. I GOT IN A LOT OF trouble. It first started when I realized I couldn't spell like the other kids. Maths and Irish were tricky, too. Irish, in particular, troubled me. Being undiagnosed with dyslexia at this early stage, and encountering a language that already had things backwards, was far too much for my mind to comprehend. Asking to go to the leithreas was as far as my Irish progressed in fourteen years. To make matters worse, my brother had one of those silver circles for excellence in Irish. It used to speak to me, shining from his school jumper. I fantasized about flushing it down the leithreas many times. But I didn't. I was very proud of him. I admired him so much. And he saw in me things he didn't possess, and he encouraged them. He was a gift.

This was the 1980s, not a time when student well-being or inclusion were top priorities. As my father was a journalist for the *Irish Times*, literature and knowledge were big commodities in the family. 'Not knowing' was not a good position to find yourself in. You would be ridiculed for it. I tried to hide the fact that something was wrong. I felt like I had a terrible secret that I had to keep hidden. I remember my father trying to teach me the alphabet; patience and sensitivity were not attributes with which he was endowed. 'Come on, you should know this at your age! What's wrong with you?' My progress in school wasn't much better. 'Oh, you're Shane's brother, I expect big things, so.'

I thought I was stupid. All the feedback was telling me I was stupid. But deep down I knew I had talent, too. There was an incongruence between my outer self and the inner self I wanted to project. So, I acted out. The last thing I wanted was for my peers to see I was stupid, so I deflected that by becoming difficult in school. I played truant, gave cheek to teachers, got in fights, anything I could to deflect from the fact that I was struggling academically. Very soon, I was labelled as 'wild'. My parents struggled to control me, school didn't know what to do with me. The two systems came together and agreed: diagnosis = wild. That description suited me. I could live with being wild. I couldn't live with being stupid.

When I was ten years old, I broke vertebrae in my lower back jumping off my neighbour's roof. We had a competition in my estate, and damned if I was going to lose. I was always very competitive. I still am. So I won, but I lost a bit, too. It was months before my parents sought medical help, because they thought I was just trying to get off school. It was my grandmother who pushed them to see a doctor when she noticed I was 'stooped'. When the doctor ran his fingers down my spine, I fainted. I woke up in traction. Lucky, by all accounts, to be able to walk. I spent weeks in hospital in traction. But I was delighted because I had no school. Wild.

To the unobservant eye, I didn't care. The reality was very different. I cared so much I was attempting to bend reality so no one could see the real me: the stupid, weak child who couldn't even manage school. That was the internal voice I developed. That was the bind I caught myself in. And I lived out that paradigm for many years.

It really wasn't until I started to use a laptop that my ability for writing started to show. My English teacher in Rochestown College, Tom O'Flaherty, always encouraged me and told me I was great at the subject. I felt I had a talent for it, but my spellings and reading told me otherwise. Even when I started to get first-class honours in college, I didn't really believe those results. The negative internalized voice was so strong that when I came in the top percentile in UCC summer exams, and the English faculty wrote to me asking me to keep on taking their subjects, I brushed it off. I told myself, 'They must be desperate for numbers.' That's the problem with these early experiences, they permeate every aspect of your life and change how you talk to yourself. Dyslexia had a voice. It spoke to me. 'You can't do that', 'You're stupid', 'Don't spell, they'll know you are stupid.'

In 2021, I wrote about my experience growing up with dyslexia in my column for the *Irish Examiner*. I was forty-four years of age. It was the first time I had ever publicly said I had dyslexia. I thought long and hard about writing the article, I questioned whether I really wanted to put it out there for everyone to see. But over the years, as a teacher and lecturer, I had met so many students who struggled with that same terrible internal voice. For many years I helped them with their voice but never revealed my own experience with it. I was terrified of being found out. I met a doctor recently who was on the verge of retiring and he explained that he was looking forward to being able to stop worrying about people finding out he was dyslexic from his handwritten prescriptions. He had spent his entire career hiding this terrible truth. That's how I felt, too. It was such a thief of my joy. I wrote the article because things had to change.

In it, I described the dyslexic voice and I mentioned how my fifth-class teacher, Brigid O'Grady, was the first person to see beyond the elaborate 'wild man' facade I had created. The next morning, as I was sitting in my clinic, I received an email from Brigid. Even now, as I write this, I can feel the emotions I experienced that afternoon reading her email. I was sobbing. Her opening line got me in the old rag and bone shop of the heart: 'I remember you well, Richard, you were a beautiful little boy.' What upset me most about that line is that I never saw myself like that. I never thought I was worthy of someone's admiration. How could I be? I was a failure, academically speaking, and a disappointment. She recalled a time when I was sitting in class trying to do an exam. She said when she spoke with me, she could see I was holding back my emotions as I looked up at her and said, 'I can't do it, I'm just a bit stupid.' I was sobbing reading this in my clinic. The email took me back into the skin of that young boy. The young pretender, who didn't care about anything, yet was crying in class because he cared so much about being stupid.

We often get caught in paradoxical behaviour. We care about something so much, we act like we don't care at all. We are so frightened of being hurt, we never allow ourselves to love, and therefore hurt ourselves constantly. We fear rejection, so we reject everything. The external environment crashes in on our thinking and robs us of joy. It certainly did that for me as a child. I didn't view myself as in any way valuable for many years.

7. How you can get sacrificed for family balance

In family therapy there is a concept known as 'homeostasis'. This means balance. No matter the family type, the personalities at play, the individual circumstances, all families have one crucial thing in common: they seek balance, a steady state of equilibrium. Balance is about the system more than the individual. The system wants to achieve and maintain a workable stability – but that can sometimes come at the expense of the individuals within that system.

Families are the most complicated systems we will ever navigate. All families have their own unique homeostasis. It is derived from the Latin word meaning 'same status'. Families constantly endeavour to keep the same status so that all members of the system are clearly defined within set parameters. This helps to make sense of the complexity of the family. If you ever wanted to visibly see homeostasis at work, watch what happens to you when you go back into the family system after a period of absence from it. You might have moved country, achieved huge things in your life, but the moment you walk back in the door of your family home, surrounded by the people you grew up with, everything you know and everything you feel about who you are disappears in that moment, because the family positions you, once again, as the youngest, the responsible eldest, et cetera. That is homeostasis at work, and it is powerful. All systems resist change, which is why homeostasis is present in family systems: it maintains the equilibrium of that family system, even if it damages those within it.

Living up to your label

It is in the drive to create and maintain balance that labels are written. This can result in limiting a child's development by assigning them a label that lasts a lifetime. If you are labelled 'sensible' or 'wild' or 'studious' or 'selfless', that label becomes your role in the system. Your role aligns with all the other assigned roles to keep the system steady and in check. You are expected to behave in that manner, always. In this way, children can easily become scapegoated in the family. If the family labels a child as 'difficult' or 'needy', the child acts that description out in order to maintain the balance of the family system. Even if the label assigned to you doesn't match your own sense of self, you can end up living up to it – or down to it – because it's expected of you.

I have seen this process of homeostasis in my clinical work, and also in my lived experience as a family member. It is powerful because it traps a child in a rigid description. I always tell parents, 'If you want your child to change, start talking about them differently.' When you talk to or about your child, how do you describe them? Homeostasis can be the breeding ground of the self-fulfilling prophecy. If you describe your child as 'weak' or 'bold', they will live that out, to sustain the balance of the family. For example, if you are the eldest daughter and were described as the sensible, dutiful child, what impact do you think that had on how you behaved in the family? There was no room for you to be anything other than that, and so you damped down certain parts of yourself, to live out the label and maintain the balance.

The danger of homeostasis is that a change in one family member forces the rest to adapt and change as well. Therefore, families can often prevent a child from changing. But families can be unaware of this process, failing to realize they are resistant to a family member's efforts to change or grow. It can be an incredibly powerful moment when this process is revealed to the family. The invisible force that has held them all so tightly in place is finally exposed, and a new balance is reached.

I met a couple many years ago when I was training as a therapist, and the woman was entirely dominated and subjugated by her husband. He was adamant that he didn't want his wife going into therapy. In my first meeting with him, he was quite aggressive towards me and told me, 'I don't believe in the work you do.' My training had taught me that I was witnessing the process of homeostasis. As the husband saw it, I was a potential disruptor to his balance.

CASE STUDY
Masking the real problem

I worked with a teenager once who was self-harming. When we explored this behaviour, she explained the tension in her family. Her mother was an alcoholic, but it wasn't spoken about. The child's self-harm was a way to keep the family in balance: she was the one with an issue, not the family. Her behaviour was deflecting all the attention away from the real problem.

I asked her, 'What would we be talking about if we weren't talking about your self-harm?'

She paused and understood what was being asked of her.

I've seen a similar phenomenon with children raised in a dysfunctional family. They will often exhibit disruptive behaviour to maintain the balance in the family. Any attempt to help the child move out of this behaviour might be rejected by the family because, if he isn't disrupting the family, then the real pathology might be revealed. A child can subconsciously act in a way that maintains the balance of the family. They do this out of love for the family unit. But in some cases the behaviour of family members is designed to hide deeper problems in the system. It might be too problematic for the system if the real problem was exposed.

The behaviour of children within families often maintains the balance of the family unit. I certainly experienced this first-hand as a depressed teenager. My father said to me one evening, 'I'll do anything to support you.' I wanted to say, 'You are the cause of my low mood.' But I didn't. I thanked him, and the homeostasis was maintained.

What you can do
The position in which we randomly find ourselves within our family system is significant. It impacts on how our parents see us, and therefore on how we see ourselves. Think about that for a moment. Where are you in the sibling hierarchy? What impact has that had on you?

Thinking of labels, did your family give you a role to perform in order to maintain balance? Who would have had to change the most if you didn't act out that role? When you find the answer to this important question, you will discover who is the keeper of the homeostasis in your family.

Think about homeostasis like this: imagine your father, mother or both set the thermostat in the house to 60° because it was freezing outside. They lock that setting, and everything is fine, but then the season changes. The temperature on the thermostat is static, unchanging, unwilling to allow for the changing season outside. You can't change the temperature, so you open windows, and leave the fridge door open. The thermostat reads the drop in temperature and reacts to maintain the set temperature by increasing the heat. In its constant vigilance to keep the balance, it might even burn itself out. That is the process of homeostasis.

Change is a process, and all homeostasis can be rewritten. The important thing to remember is that families are generally resistant to change. But it is all about feedback. When you want to change how you are perceived in the family, or your role within the family system, remember it will take time. Families like to label, and if the label you were given is no longer fit for purpose, or perhaps was never fit for purpose, you will have to give that feedback repeatedly to your family members until the system starts to reorient its perception and labelling of you. This takes time, but change can and does happen.

YOUR GENOGRAM

Let's go back to your genogram.

1. Who created the homeostasis in your family?
   Remember, the way to discover this is to identify who would have had to change the most if you didn't play your role. Write it in next to their name.

2. Think about what labels were given to you by your family. Write them next to your name. Did you live them out? If you were labelled as 'the sensible one', being wild or adventurous might not have been on offer to you. You had to be sensible to maintain the equilibrium of the system. Maybe you still fulfil that role in adult life?

3. Think about everyone in your family system and what role they played to maintain the balance of that system. Write their roles next to their names.

4. Now think about your relationship with yourself: if you stopped living out those old paradigms about who you are, what would need to change? Write it down on your genogram.

8. The unforgettable lessons of fear

Fear is an emotional response to a perceived threat, and it has been a very important response in our survival as a species. We needed it in order to protect ourselves from environmental threats in our early evolution. If we assumed the noise in the bush was benign and nothing to worry about, we wouldn't have made it very far as a species. Fear is important, and we all feel it from time to time.

I hear so many experts talking about living without fear, and I think it's very unhelpful. Fear is a natural and important human experience. When people are told they can live without fear, it only serves to further enhance their sense of failure when they feel it and are motivated by it. Learning to harness your fear and work through it is a far more beneficial way to think about fear. If you were getting on to a flight and the pilot said, 'We don't have any safety warning system operating today, but we don't expect any problems flying over the Alps,' would you get on that flight? Your feelings of fear would motivate you to make the right decision. So, we all feel fear, and with very good reasons.

That said, our first lesson in how we should manage fear came from our parents. Their behaviour modelled for us how to respond to negative stimuli. Think about your parents, and how they behaved in stressful situations. Do you act the same way? Those modelled responses become embedded into our subconscious, only to replay in adulthood when we experience fear or stress. This can become a disempowering experience if we feel stuck repeating behaviours we know are not helpful.

Hot and cold cognition

Hot and cold cognition are interesting processes that occur in all of us.

When you have a disagreement with someone, or someone cuts in front of you in traffic, and you respond with aggression or anger, that is hot cognition. Anger is fear's antidote: your emotional response when you perceive a threat. Fight, flight or freeze are generally the favoured responses when cognition is hot. The experience stays down in the threat area in the brain and doesn't get pushed up to the neocortex for analysis.

When you experience the same negative stimuli and you take your time to respond in a considered way, and don't become irate or angry, that is cold cognition.

It is easier to fall into hot cognition because that is generally how we were primed to respond to negative stimuli. Passive aggression is one way to get our cognition hot. Let's say you believe a family member always says negative things about you. You are at a dinner with family and something negative is said. You become irate, based more on what you feel 'always happens' than on what has just happened. What do you do? Say something hurtful back? Perhaps later you analyse it and think, *I wish I had acted better*. You snapped back, and they said, 'Relax, I was only joking,' and then you looked like the mad one!

If you were to respond with cold cognition, what would that sound like? What would happen if you said, 'What is the joke there? I don't get it. Can you explain it?' Now your cognition is cold and you are a formidable opponent. They might be slower to make a jibe the next time, because they know you won't react with emotion but with intellect. They will treat you with more care and be less likely to fling casual comments your way. That's a definite win.

Although it might be hard, we can all cool down our cognition when it becomes heated. It takes intentional behaviour to disrupt the old negative behaviour patterns. But that's all they are, familiar patterns. When you can control your hot cognition through understanding what your default responses are, that can make you incredibly powerful.

What does fear do to the body?

Fear reaction starts in the brain and spreads through the body quickly, preparing and making adjustments for the best defence or flight reaction. The fear response starts in a region of the brain called the amygdala. Located in the temporal lobe, the amygdala is dedicated to detecting the danger levels of an external threat. Information comes into the body through the senses and is processed rapidly by the amygdala so that the body can prepare for an immediate survival response.

The amygdala is an important part of the human story. It helps us to make sense of the environment around us, but also to make quick judgement calls on social engagement. When it is excited, it activates a stress hormone that prepares the body to be more effective in that particular situation. It is constantly reading the environment and pushing information up to the prefrontal cortex to assess the perceived threat level. It is this interplay between the amygdala, the hippocampus and the prefrontal cortex that maintains balance, or homeostasis, within the body. When that system is interrupted, the balance shifts and all extraneous functioning is shut down so the body has all the energy it needs to survive.

But what happens when that thinking part of the brain becomes disrupted through chaotic childhood experiences? Well, the brain cannot make those context calls, leaving the emotional brain to drive the response. That is when things can get very tricky for a person. In my clinical experience, people who have had traumatic childhood experiences have had their processing system disrupted by the constant chaos in their life, and information does not move up to be processed, therefore any threat results in a chaotic, emotional reaction.

Of course, this chaotic reaction returns to a steady balance, but it will become triggered again by any negative or associated stimuli, and then the process starts all over again. This cycle traps the person in the belief that they are powerless against their anxiety. When their cognition becomes hot, they struggle to cool it down. This means hot cognition is steering their response to threat.

Think about yourself: how do you respond when your cognition becomes hot/emotionally led? Generally, we tend to fall back on those behaviours and coping mechanisms that were modelled for us by our parents. How did your parents respond to stress? What did they do when their cognition became hot? The chances are that you are simply replaying those responses, over and over again, because that is what is coded into your memory as a useful response. But is it useful?

I try to be very intentional about my stress responses in front of my children. Sometimes I role-play being under pressure when I'm not, so that I can role-model healthy responses for them. I pretend I can't find the car keys and I have an important meeting to make. I go through cold cognition steps to model it for them. I think out loud: 'When I came in, where did I put the keys? No, they are not there. Okay, so where did I go after I came in? What coat was I wearing? Oh, great, I have them.' And I leave. No drama, no fuss, problem solved.

I certainly wasn't always like that. I used to respond to those situations in a very negative way, pulling the couch apart, raising my voice in panic, shouting to no one how I was going to miss the meeting because someone had decided to torment me by hiding the keys. I had witnessed this type of behaviour my whole life. I had heard my father describe, in very vivid imagery, how the entire world was working against him as he tore the house apart trying to find where he left the car keys the night before. It was always a chaotic scene, and I replicated that for a short period of my adult life. Later, I realized it was entirely unhelpful, and I trained myself to stay calm and cool down my cognition. And it works! I have seen the impact this modelling has on my own children – when they are late and searching for something they need, I can hear my daughter working through cold cognition to find it. Again, no drama, no fuss, problem solved.

Fear is learned

We learn fear through personal experiences. Let's just say you were attacked by an aggressive dog, or you observed someone being attacked by an aggressive dog, this would provoke a strong reaction from you next time a strange dog approached you. Your amygdala would fire the warning, preparing you to fight or run, and your thinking brain would confirm that threat by evoking the memory of the previous attack. Then you would respond accordingly, probably by running away and shouting for help.

It's also the case that we can learn fear from other people. I often find myself bemused at the fear response provoked by a wasp. The majority of people have never been stung, but the fear a wasp provokes is fascinating. You could be sitting with the most rational, sensible person and all of a sudden they are dancing, waving their hands like they are on fire, because a wasp has entered their orbit. When you ask, they confess they have never been stung in their lives – so why the big reaction? This fear has been learned and passed on through language. Our parents teach us what to be afraid of. That means we can be afraid of things we've never experienced. The mere mention of a perceived threat can cause all sorts of distress. But it's very real. Once triggered, the thinking brain is shut off by the imminent threat of attack and the emotional response takes over. This is borrowed or inherited fear.

—

CASE STUDY
Held prisoner by fear

I worked with a couple who brought their young daughter to me because she was refusing to go outside the house. The couple were in their forties when their daughter was born, having struggled for many years to conceive. When Sarah was born, they were overjoyed by the miracle of her life but also very fearful that something terrible might happen. She was premature, and they feared she was weak.

The mother explained that her own mother was a particularly nervous parent and didn't allow them the space to explore as children. She said her mother always expected something terrible to happen to them. Now, she explained, she was the same, and now her child didn't want to go outside because something terrible might happen. Fear had been handed down the generations. Nobody was thriving. They were stuck in this fear position, terrified of the world.

Slowly, I prescribed the parents bringing their daughter to the park and letting her play in the playground. Then she went on playdates without them, and eventually they all learned to relax and become more comfortable in their life together.

—

When we experience dysfunction and frightening things with the people in our lives, especially with the people who raised us, it can disrupt the thinking part of the brain. The system is hijacked by fear and becomes inconsistent. The key factor here is our sense of control. When we are able to recognize what is and isn't a real threat, and to confidently label an experience accordingly, we feel in control. That perception of control is vital to how we experience and respond to fear. When we overcome the initial fight-or-flight rush, we are often left feeling satisfied, reassured of our safety and more confident in our ability to confront the things that initially scared us.

What you can do

Is there a memory that you feel is significant in your life, one that provokes fear? Is there a memory from your childhood that replays regularly in your mind? What have you told yourself about who you are because of that memory?

Could you 'rewrite' that memory and think about it in a more positive way? If you did that with your memory and rewrote it, what would be the new, positive message you could take away from it?

YOUR GENOGRAM

Let's go back to your genogram and record how your parents modelled responses to fear and stress.

1. What was your parents' default response when they became fearful or anxious? Was that response helpful to resolving the situation, or not?
2. Ask yourself, do you now enact those same responses? Write down your default responses to fear and stress.
3. Consider whether those responses are helpful to you. If not, what responses would serve you better?

9. *Comfortably numb – the power of positive feedback loops*

When I think of all the issues I have met over the years, all the causes of suffering in people's lives, I am forced to conclude that positive feedback loops are one of the leading causes of distress.

A positive feedback loop is anything you use to make yourself feel better in the immediate present but which spirals your life into chaos in the long-term. For example, I had a client who fainted in school one day and became worried he would faint again and embarrass himself in front of his peers. As a result, he refused to go to school. Staying home made that fear go away, but it also dramatically increased his overall sense of fear. He began to dread the idea of school. The thing he used to manage his fear – staying home – was the thing that was feeding his fear. We broke this behaviour quite quickly by showing him how that fear naturally left once he was in school. It took about four weeks to disrupt that positive feedback loop and then his life went back to normal.

Every system will orient itself towards homeostasis, balance. A positive feedback loop works to disrupt that natural state of equilibrium. Positive feedback loops enhance or accelerate behaviour that is not helpful. They are at the core of habit formation. Put simply: when a person performs a behaviour and it impacts the reward centre of the brain (the person feels better for doing that behaviour, for example gambling, alcohol, infidelity), the person's motivation to perform the behaviour increases because a reward is expected. This pushes the person further and further away from healthy balance as they seek out more of the same behaviour in order to feel good.

—

CASE STUDY
Trying to control the uncontrollables

I had a client recently tell me that she spent an entire flight to New York with her feet held off the ground because she believed that if her feet touched the floor of the plane, it would crash. I asked her what it had felt like when the plane landed at JFK. She laughed as she told me that she felt proud she had saved the entire plane. Of course, she knew she hadn't. But her fear had forced her to attempt to control a situation over which she actually had no control.

I told her the story about the English psychologist who was carrying out a study on anxiety. In one of his visits to an in-patient psychiatric unit, he observed a woman clapping her hands repeatedly. When he asked her why she was clapping her hands she explained, 'It keeps the elephants away.' When he informed her that there were no elephants in England, she declared, 'See, it works!'

When I told my client that elephant story, she laughed and shook her head. 'I know, I know,' she said, 'I'm crazy.' I explained that she wasn't crazy, just using hyper-rationality to manage anxiety. She agreed with me.

Two weeks later, she was travelling to Lanzarote. I asked her, 'Please, on that flight, can you also save everyone and keep your feet off the ground?' She looked at me as if I had lost my mind. I was prescribing the very thing she thought made her appear crazy.

A month later, she bounced into the clinic, exclaiming that she had been cured. She wasn't cured – because she wasn't sick to begin with, she was just running an old loop that had worked when she was a child and felt anxious. But it did not fit her adult life.

So, how had she broken the loop? Together, we had identified where in her childhood she had developed that particular response. But that was only the starting point. She then had to intentionally disrupt it in order to create change – and she would have to keep repeating that disruption if she wanted to see lasting change. She had been obsessively trying to control things that were out of her control, and I simply used a paradoxical intervention to bring her to realize that.

She believed that her solution – keeping her feet off the ground – brought a positive outcome, which was reinforced for her when the plane didn't crash. But the very solution she was using to make her feel in control was making her behaviour spiral out of control. She was stuck in a positive feedback loop. I gave her a simple mantra to say: 'Take control of not having control, and that will give you control.' This is a very helpful mantra if you are bombarded by perfectionist ideas, or you desperately want to control every aspect of your life.

—

It sounds funny, but getting caught in a system of thought like my client who believed she could save the plane from crashing can have serious consequences. And it's extremely common – many of us get caught in this type of bind. We believe that worry causes a positive outcome. Worry is our armour, and we don't want to move through the world without it. But in truth, worry is the antithesis of joy.

Taking control of not having control is what gives you control

There is so much of our world that is beyond our control. Trying to control everything puts you into a tight bind. I often show clients what I mean by asking them to take a pen in their hand and squeeze it as hard as they can. I leave them there, fist extended, face going red. I ask them what it feels like. They generally respond by saying, 'Sore, unsustainable.' Then I ask them to turn the hand over and open it. They explain that this is much better, much easier, sustainable.

This exercise gives them a physical representation of what they are bringing into their life by living in this tightly wound-up position. They are putting huge effort, energy and time into trying to control things, to be permanently in control, but it's achieving nothing – life happens all around you, whether your fist is curled up tight or opened out. There are so many things you simply can't make happen or stop happening.

When your thinking and behaviour are ruled by fear, this is the point it brings you to – where your whole self is balled up tight, trying to make the world stop spinning on its axis. You can't achieve this. The only thing you can do is accept that you cannot control everything. In a paradoxical switch, accepting this realization will give you the control you crave. It gives you the ultimate control, because you will no longer be attempting to control the uncontrollables in your life. You are freed from the desire to control.

Phobic behaviours

If you feel anxious and you don't know why, you may start to avoid what you believe caused it, such as crowds, going out, school. This is how you can develop phobic behaviours. These are behaviours that are based in fear. When we feel fear, we generally have three responses: control the situation, avoid the situation or look for reassurance. Phobic people use avoidance to manage their fear. The more you avoid, the more you believe avoiding is helping your levels of anxiety. However, the avoidance is actually increasing your anxiety and exacerbating its other effects, such as a sense of isolation and disconnection. This can lead to despair.

—

CASE STUDY
Scratching the scab

A teenage girl came to therapy because she had soiled herself in class and now was terrified that she would do it again, which would be incredibly embarrassing. She started to avoid school. She explained that the day it happened, she had drunk too much water at lunch break and was too shy to ask to go to the toilet. Now she feared it could happen again. She was stuck, just like the boy who had fainted and was fearful it would happen again. Her response, like his, was to avoid the stress-inducing situation.

She was a high-performing student and had always enjoyed the school environment. Her parents were very concerned because this phobia had come out of nowhere. This once vibrant school-loving girl had become a shadow of her former self, and her parents were extremely worried that something more serious was disturbing her.

In our initial conversation, I could tell a positive feedback loop was at the core of this helpless and unhelpful way of looking at her situation. Her fear had provoked an avoiding behaviour, which fed the fear further, so she became reliant on avoiding and couldn't see any other option. She was trapped in a recursive loop of behaviour. She was moving further and further from balance and felt utterly trapped.

When I discussed it with her parents, they described how they had recently started to pull up around the corner from the school and try to coax her out of the car. Most days, it didn't work. I immediately disrupted this approach and told them to pull up in front of the school – as they always had – to let her out, and then drive off. No hesitation.

The next week, they reported that they had done this, and she had gone into school. She told me she had felt anxious in school at first, but that quickly passed by the second class.

The next week, I asked her to walk to school, as she had always done previously, and she did it. Slowly, each week, we deconstructed the positive feedback loop. Within five sessions, her parents described the relief they felt having their daughter returned to them. Her confidence was back, she was no longer avoiding school, and she was thriving once again.

She was a formidable client to work with. She refused to allow herself to be trapped by her thinking. An image she found very helpful when I was working with her was the image of a scab. I told her to picture a cut on her arm, then to imagine it as it healed. The blood has coagulated slightly and now it's itchy. The question I posed was: what do you do? You can scratch it, and in that immediate moment feel good, but the cut now goes deeper and the blood has to coagulate again, making the cut more inflamed and itchier. What do you do now? Do you scratch it again, deeper and deeper, until it becomes a scar, a constant source of irritation? If you had not scratched it (i.e., if you had confronted your fear) and not attempted to relieve the itchiness and pain, it would have healed and gone away rapidly. She found this incredibly helpful. Whenever she felt anxious, she thought, 'I'm not scratching it. Let it heal.' A simple image created a new way of managing her fear and brought balance and harmony back into her life.

—

Breaking the loop

We all know what we like and what makes us feel good, but sometimes we don't know why we do things that get in the way of making us feel good. For example, I was working with a client recently and I got him to write a list of his responses to having a bad day. He put down the following:

When I feel low and in a bad mood, I:

- retreat from people
- stop exercising
- eat badly
- stay in bed all day.

I asked him to make a list of what life is like when he feels good. He wrote the following:

When life is good, I enjoy:

- hanging out with friends
- exercising, going to the gym
- eating healthy food/having a positive body image
- being productive.

I then asked him to write out what he needed to stop doing if he wanted to improve his well-being. He wrote the following:

The things that stop me feeling better are:

- retreating from people
- no exercising
- eating badly
- staying in bed all day.

From this you can see that he is caught in a positive feedback loop. The things he does when he feels low are the very things that push him away from feeling better. With that client, this was one of the most profound breakthroughs he had with regard to his mental health. He stopped doing things that made him feel low and started doing more of what made him feel good. Very simple, but very effective.

I often work with drug addicts and I ask them to describe their feelings just before they buy drugs. I can see they really don't want to do that. They are reluctant, because they know that once they become aware of those feelings, it will ruin the buzz of 'scoring' the next time. They will be conscious of those false feelings.

What you can do

Think about your own responses to not feeling good. What do you do? You must become conscious of what you do in response to not feeling good. And you must learn to lean into the positive behaviours that will counteract this.

Now, write out your lists:

- What do you do when you're having a bad day?
- What is life like when you are having a great day?
- What do you do that stops you from having a great day?

Compare the two and make a checklist to see if you sometimes get caught in a positive feedback loop.

YOUR GENOGRAM

Go back to your genogram and look at all the information you have filled in at this point.

1. Next to your parents' names, write in their responses to feeling happy and unhappy. Are they also at play in your life?
2. Consult your list of your behaviours in response to having a good/bad day. What patterns can you see? Can you see changes that need to be made?

10. *How you talk to yourself matters*

There is nothing more important than the self-talk that goes on in your head. What is that voice like? Is it supportive of you? Championing you and encouraging you to succeed? Or does it criticize you? Say terrible things about your ability? Put you down constantly, rule over you like some ruthless despot?

I often speak to that voice in the clinic, and I hear what it says to the person. I am always struck by the levels of nastiness that voice can sink to.

CASE STUDY
'You'd be better off dead'

I worked with a teenage girl recently who described her inner voice talking to her: 'You're ugly, your ears are too big and your nose is weird. Your legs are like men's legs and you are false and pretend to be happy but you couldn't be happy looking like you do, you'd be better off dead.' Her internal voice was causing huge distress in her life, potentially threatening her survival.

In our conversation, I asked her if she had ever seen a really ugly girl. She admitted she hadn't. I asked if she did, would she say those words to her. She admitted she wouldn't. Then I asked why she felt comfortable saying those terrible things to herself. She broke down, sobbing, and recalled a time when girls isolated her and bullied her very badly in school and on social media.

The school had made things far worse by calling the girls into the office and ordering them to stop calling her names. After that, they started calling her an 'ugly rat'. Their tormenting intensified, but she didn't tell anyone in case it would cause more problems. They'd hide her school bag and make calls to her phone telling her she'd be better off dead. It really was one of the worst cases of bullying I had ever witnessed.

Slowly, we started to unpack their voices from inside her head. Her internalized voice had been corrupted by that experience. But she started to realize that those girls were wrong, that she wasn't ugly, that their behaviour was ugly. Her internal voice slowly started to improve.

—

We all need to have a better relationship with ourselves, we all need to have more compassion for ourselves. We are human, imperfect, and trying our best to get things right.

The power of internalized beliefs

A number of years ago, I was the year head in a fee-paying school. This meant I was in charge of discipline. One student, who had been reasonably well behaved up until this point, started to act out in fifth year, and I was called upon to intervene. This is his story.

—

CASE STUDY
Trapped in a self-fulfilling prophecy

I noticed very early on that this student – I'll call him John – repeatedly got himself in trouble in a classroom where the teacher was particularly strict. If ever there was a teacher to avoid annoying, it was this one. That struck me immediately.

One day, as I was coming through the yard, the strict teacher stopped me and in a very irate tone told me I had to discipline John because he was disrupting his class. He told me that he expected me to act with speed and authority. In short, he wanted the student suspended. It was obvious that he was at the end of his tether.

Later that day, I spoke with John. He was the inscrutable type, didn't give much away. He was sullen, monosyllabic. Typical teenager in many ways. But he was also quite rude when I spoke to him.

RICHARD: You seem to be getting into trouble a lot in
    Mr P's classroom, can you tell me what you think is
    happening?

JOHN: Nothing much, the usual.

RICHARD: What's the usual?

JOHN: You know the way he is.

RICHARD: What way is that?

JOHN: Angry, shouts about everything. He needs to chill.

RICHARD: Okay, I'll ask him to chill. (*John laughs.*) Are you chilled?

JOHN: Oh yeah. Are you?

RICHARD: Not as much as I used to be.

JOHN: You should chill more.

RICHARD: What does being chilled look like?

JOHN: Ah you know, 4.20 relaxed, man. [*4.20 refers to smoking hash.*]

RICHARD: I can sense you're annoyed and being a little provocative. Is this the attitude that gets you into trouble?

JOHN: Yeah.

RICHARD: What would we call it?

JOHN: Dunno.

RICHARD: Would cheekiness be the right adjective?

JOHN: Probably.

RICHARD: Is there anything else it could be called?

JOHN: Nah, cheekiness is good.

RICHARD: Can I ask you to do something a little weird?

JOHN: (*He is looking up now through his fringe.*) Depends.

RICHARD: I want to talk to your Cheekiness.

JOHN: Okay. Whatever you're into. (*Laughing awkwardly.*)

RICHARD: So, I'm not talking to John now, I'm speaking with Cheekiness.

JOHN: Grand.

RICHARD: Hi, Cheekiness, thanks for coming into the room. How are you?

CHEEKINESS: Grand.

RICHARD: When did John first notice you were there?

CHEEKINESS: Dunno – first year.

RICHARD: What was going on for John at that point?

CHEEKINESS: He was a bit of a wimp.

RICHARD: What do you mean a wimp?

CHEEKINESS: Scared, eating lunch in the toilet.

RICHARD: So what did you do to help?

CHEEKINESS: Ah you know, started making jokes, mocking teachers.

RICHARD: What did your peers think?

CHEEKINESS: They liked it. I mean, no one came near John to fight or nothing.

RICHARD: So you protected John?

CHEEKINESS: Yeah, I did.

RICHARD: What did your teachers think of you?

CHEEKINESS: They didn't like me. Fuck 'em.

(I decided to use a few circular questions to bring his family in.)

RICHARD: What does your father think of your Cheekiness?

(There is a pause. John looks down at his shoes.)

JOHN: Nothing.

At this point the atmosphere changed in the room. John's appearance changed and he almost became smaller in his chair, like the air was sucked out of him.

RICHARD: What would your Cheekiness like to say to your father?

(A long pause.)

JOHN: Come home.

(At this point he is crying. He is a big young man and he is sobbing in the chair in front of me.)

RICHARD: What are your tears saying?

JOHN: Come home, Dad, stop working so hard.

In the conversation that followed, John explained that his father was a taxi driver. He was attending this fee-paying school and his father had to work to pay the fees. This was causing him to be away from home a lot. It was putting pressure on his mother and the talk at home often drifted to how much the father was sacrificing for his son's education. Even his brothers were getting at him to study because his father wasn't there. John held a belief that he wasn't intelligent and so wasn't worth all this effort. In his analysis, the only way out of the bind was to get expelled so that he could go to a 'normal' school and the pressure on everyone wouldn't be so great. He was trying, in his own way, to bring his belief to life. And it was working.

—

I have met so many young men like John; they hold a destructive, negative idea about themselves, and they bring it into life. They form the idea, cling tight to it, and their self-talk revolves around it, constantly reinforcing it inside their heads. Even though they're afraid of it, they start behaving in a way that will make it happen. It becomes a self-fulfilling prophecy – and it can cause so much pain and suffering.

—

CASE STUDY
Killing the thing you love the most

Recently, I had a middle-aged client come to me because he had separated from his wife. He explained that she had left him after he'd embarked on an affair. When we started to unpack why he'd brought this negativity into his life when he was happily married, the paradigm or internalized belief became clear.

I know many people will think, *You can't be happily married and have an affair*. I understand how you could think of an affair like that. But maybe it's more a case of not being happy in yourself, if you have an affair when you are happily married. Of course, people have affairs because they are hedonistic and only do what they want to, without consideration for the outcome. But my client's story had another layer: he was devastated at losing the one person who gave his life meaning.

As we explored it, he described how his parents' separation devastated him when he was a child. He painted a very sad image of himself watching from his bedroom window as his dad packed the car. When I asked him what that experience meant to him, he said, 'Everything turns to shit.' He repeated it and said it had become his mantra. He also described how he'd always believed his wife was far better than him and believed she would eventually leave him. He spoke about his wedding morning, how he asked his mother to call his future mother-in-law to make sure his fiancée was going to turn up at the church.

The affair, as he described it, was a way of protecting himself. He had a 'get out of jail card' when it all eventually, inevitably, turned to shit. He could say, 'Sure, I had an affair, I didn't really love her anyway,' when she figured out he wasn't good enough for her.

The sadness and pain in his conversation were difficult to witness.

—

This is the most profound example of the self-fulfilling prophecy I have met in my clinic. In this man's desperate attempt to protect himself, he destroyed the one thing he valued most. The paradigm he'd developed as he watched his father walk out of his life was being manifested in his reality.

Our fear of things turning out badly can cause us to behave in ways that make sure things turn out badly, thus confirming the truth of our belief.

What you can do

What ideas do you hold about yourself that you are bringing into your life? Write them out and challenge them. Once you become aware of your internalized beliefs, it is impossible to ignore them.

Think about some of your bad habits. What are the ones that really disrupt your life? No longer allow them to manifest themselves in your life. Prove them wrong.

YOUR GENOGRAM

Look back at your genogram and the information you have filled in so far about your parents.

1. What ideas do you think your parents held about themselves? How have these been transmitted to you? To your siblings?
2. Self-talk is frequently negative and destructive. It judges us, and tells us our efforts are never good enough. Next to your parents' names, write a compassionate and supportive observation about their parenting.
3. Now, write something supportive and encouraging next to your siblings' names. Next to your own. Remember, no one is perfect and gets it right all the time.

PART FIVE

Addiction, Separation and Family Dysfunction

I KNOW I WENT THROUGH A LOT AS A YOUNG BOY. IT WASN'T always obvious who I would become. At times, I didn't know whether it would work out for me, or not. I had dreams and aspirations but often didn't help myself. I didn't value myself, and there were times when my behaviour could have resulted in a very tragic outcome.

When I was living with my parents, it didn't really feel like I was living with abuse, it was simply my reality. I felt trapped, at times hopeless, but there was plenty of fun in there, too. I have often met that same mixed dynamic among the clients in my clinic. I've met children who are incredibly confused about the family they are living in. We tend to think that a dysfunctional family system is in a state of constant turmoil, but that isn't always the case.

For my part, I adored my grandmother and she gave me a strong sense of security. She was such joy to be around. At night, when I'd come home from a nightclub, I'd go into her room, lie on her bed and chat about the night. She'd ask me did I meet any nice girls and we'd laugh and joke until early morning. She'd tell me about her life as a young girl growing up in Cork, the dances she went to and how she fell in love with a Cork hurler. Those moments were special. My grandmother died in 2006, but I can still hear her voice in my ear. She is always there, driving me on. When my youngest daughter was ill, I could hear her telling me everything would be okay: 'Don't worry, boy, she'll be fine.' I know she would have been so proud of the fact that I have three daughters. That can be one of the great sorrows of life, not being able to share things with people who genuinely loved you.

When I was around sixteen years old, a friend gave me a pill late one evening after Sir Henry's nightclub. I'm not sure I really knew what it was, but I took it all the same. I had impulse control issues in those days. What followed was one of the worst experiences of my life. I started to hallucinate about the Devil. I remember standing in the chipper and the words of the menu started to spell out my name and fall down like tears from the menu board. I knew I was in trouble.

My friend dropped me home. I went up to my bedroom, the stairs like mighty Kilimanjaro. I was under the covers, terrified, the

Grim Reaper outside my window, calling me, socks dancing in the linen basket. Next thing I knew, I was down with my grandmother. She wrapped me in her blanket and calmed me down. I told her I'd had a bad burger. 'Jesus,' she declared to my shaking and incoherent ramblings, 'that must have been some burger.' For weeks she would joke with me, 'For the love of God, don't have a burger on the way home.'

Another time, coming home from a friend's house in December, I passed the Douglas Christmas tree, shining in all its splendour. I had a thought that it would be nice to have one of those lights in my bedroom for Christmas. Before I knew it, I was up the tree, unscrewing one of the bulbs, only to be interrupted by the local garda asking me what I was doing. I had no reply. He brought me home to my parents. Luckily for me, they were out. My grandmother answered the door, and seeing the dejected shadow following the garda, she didn't miss a beat. 'Oh, what has he done now?' The garda explained that I had been stealing Christmas tree lights. 'Don't you worry, Garda, I'll punish my son.' My head raised. I could see the look on the garda's face. He was far too polite to ask, but it was written all over him. My grandmother was around seventy-six years old at the time, and she was an old-looking seventy-six. I was twelve. The miraculous conception. The garda thanked her for punishing me and got back into his car, looking incredulously at the both of us as he left. As she closed the door she said, with a huge smile, 'I think we fooled him, boy.' What a gift she was.

Those moments sustain me now as an adult. But I also recall moments when things were difficult, and how we managed as a family. I wonder what it must have been like for her, to witness her son-in-law struggle with addiction. She admired him, even loved him. He was good to her, no doubt about that. But she was in the chaos, too. I find myself wondering about her experience, how she felt. The only time I ever really fought with her was when I caught herself and her sister ringing my father after he'd left the family. She was asking him to come back. I regret that fight, but I felt like she had betrayed us by doing that. But we got over it and were great friends through life.

We had a good family in many ways, but it was incredibly dysfunctional in other ways. My father let us all down. The loss and devastation he brought into our lives was needless. The impact it had on my early adult life was terrible. The loss of childhood. The endless evenings I sat in my bedroom trying to figure out what we could do to get out of the cycle we were stuck in. The hopelessness I felt.

And yet, we didn't sink under it. In fact, it motivated all of us to strive to achieve something in life. My brothers are remarkable people, hard workers, talented and generous. At this point in life, I find myself feeling incredibly sorry for my father. What he missed out on. The love he squandered and lost. The family occasions we share now as adults, from which he is absent. I talk with him from time to time. Sadness always engulfs me after the conversation. He was a talented, generous person, too. He struggled in his own life and used alcohol to manage his feelings, and it destroyed his humanity.

I was very angry with my father in those early days. To bring my grandmother into his chaos at the end of her life was unforgivable to me at that time. If I had met him walking down Patrick Street in my early twenties, it wouldn't have gone well for either of us. I was a ball of rage. It is so unhealthy to live like that. His legacy in those early years was dark. I was closed off, unreachable. We didn't mention his name for years. If we spoke about him, we called him 'your man'. It took me a long time before I called him by his name. But it was an important moment when I did. I had to forgive him for all the madness he brought into our lives.

I had to forgive myself, too, for bringing chaos into my own life as a young adult. I spoke very badly to myself in those days. Growing up in dysfunction changes how you talk to yourself and how you view the world. Later, once that voice improved, I started to work my way out of where I was. I understood that I could easily replicate my father's story, but I really didn't want any more chaos in my life, and so my life trajectory started to change. I always wanted children, and I never wanted to hurt them. I wanted to be who I said I was. The closer I got to living that, the happier I became.

My family was not perfect. I have yet to meet a perfect family. We struggled with my father's addiction and his separation from my mother, but we had lovely moments, too. My father was a lot of things in my life. But I know I am the person I am today because of my father, my mother, my grandmother, my brothers. That experience made me resilient. It made me resourceful. It led me to understand that I can rely on myself and that I can manage whatever comes into my life. When you feel like that, you are powerful.

11.   Addiction and the family

When you consume alcohol or drugs in an attempt to stave off a negative experience or memory, you push your life further and further away from equilibrium. And it has a profound impact on everyone around you.

I grew up in a house where addiction was present. I witnessed, first-hand, the devastation alcohol abuse brings into the life of an addict. In my experience, personally and clinically, I have seen how it shrinks a person's life down into nothing. My father had such a huge career, he was respected and talented. I admired him in so many ways. He was also, by all accounts, a good father in the early days of his married life. But drink destroyed all that. It warped his personality, made him deeply unhappy in his life, and took away everything that was good and wholesome. That is a lot to give away for a substance. The Grant Study (an eighty-year longitudinal study by Harvard University on human happiness and life satisfaction) teaches us that the depth and health of relationships with those you love is the greatest predictor of life satisfaction. In other words, meaning in life is all about your connection to others. As far as I could see, alcohol had disrupted and destroyed my father's relationships with those he loved and, most importantly, with himself.

Living with someone who is prone to rage and wild mood swings is a very unsettling thing to experience. I never knew the man I would meet in the morning at breakfast. He could be nice and funny, or incredibly aggressive and dogmatic. He often violently knocked a piece of toast out of my hand because 'it was [his] brown bread'. Those were daily experiences that I became almost immune to. But one of the most humiliating moments in my life happened when I was sixteen years old. Coming home one evening with my friends, there was a Garda car parked outside my house. I immediately thought something had happened to my grandmother. I ran up to the house, but my mother told me to go back out with my friends. I knew then that it had to be something to do with my father. The panic on her face, the embarrassment she felt, it all pointed to my father.

Later that week, I found out exactly what it was all about. My father was driving while drunk and had knocked down a motorcyclist and fled the scene. Cork is such a small place and it turned out that I knew the brother of the motorcyclist. I have never felt such shame as I did when he told me what had happened and that my dad was 'a scumbag for leaving'. I felt protective of my father but also deeply ashamed that a parent could do something like that. There were many moments like this over the course of my adolescence, all of which made a deep impact on my soul.

There was my eighteenth birthday, which he missed entirely, claiming he was out chasing a story about some doctor who had taken explicit images of his patients. I remember that evening so clearly. I always hated my birthday, I never wanted to celebrate it. I think it came from those moments. I developed the belief that it would inevitably be a disappointment – I knew I'd be let down. I remember walking down the road with friends, thinking how unbelievable it was that my parents hadn't even really wished me a happy birthday, when a car pulled up. I thought it was my family. The excitement quickly disappeared when I realized it wasn't them – and I felt foolish for thinking it might be. I didn't see my father for days. He didn't know it was my birthday. His story about the immoral doctor was nonsense. In reality, he was drunk somewhere. His life was out of control, and we were all dragged along for the terrible ride.

When we were young, my father used to always impress on us how important it was to tell the truth. And now everything in his life was a lie. That's what addiction does to your life, and to the lives of the people caught in your orbit. Everything spirals out of control so rapidly. I had always thought that alcoholics were those people I saw on the street, homeless and destitute. I never thought an alcoholic could be someone who brings you to school or has a good job. We certainly didn't use the term 'alcoholic' for a long time in my family.

That's another devastating aspect of growing up with addiction: secrets become a huge part of your life. The family becomes a secretive place, where no outsider is allowed in. Everyone in the family becomes guarded, closed.

I clearly remember going on a retreat with the secondary school I was going to, Rochestown College. One of the speakers described his childhood growing up with an alcoholic parent. It was my story. It was the first time I realized my father was an addict. I had suspected it up to that point, but now I knew for sure. I wanted to go up to the speaker at the end, but I was too embarrassed, and I also didn't want to let anyone know what was going on in my family. It used to gall me when one of my teachers would show me an article my father had written in the newspaper. The pretence was all too much. But I still never said anything to anyone. Everyone in the family unit held that secret tightly – we were all bound up in it.

Living with stress

Growing up with an addicted parent is a very damaging experience. It changes how you see the world. Research shows that it can change the neurochemistry in the brain. A robust body of research has demonstrated that prolonged or repeated exposure to stress and trauma can have serious negative consequences for physical and mental health, particularly when stress is experienced early in development. The research is clear that early trauma can cause negative functional outcomes across lifespan, such as inability to emotionally regulate, dissociative disorder, depression and post-traumatic stress disorder (PTSD). Early trauma can cause potential structural and functional alterations within the hippocampus, the prefrontal cortex and the amygdala.

What I have noticed in my own clinical practice is that clients who grew up in dysfunction often struggle to process the level of threat they are experiencing. They have grown up in a constant state of alarm, so when they experience the slightest stress they are unable to process the level of threat. They become confused and frightened. Think of it like a person visiting a zoo and not understanding the function of the barriers. They see a lion and cannot process the fact that they are safe – all they can see is the danger, and they panic. There is no context or application of logic. The information doesn't get pushed up to the neocortex for analysis, it stays down in the threat area of the amygdala. It means they are living in a near-constant state of stress. Living like this can make you less optimistic, less able to experience joy, and can even impact your choice of partner.

Another aspect that I see in my clinic – and I experienced this first-hand in adolescence – is dissociative disorder. The brain has an incredible ability to tolerate stress and trauma, but one of its protective behaviours is to cause the person to disassociate, or to 'split', from themself. This does not mean they are schizophrenic; it's not like having a dual personality that develops on its own. It means that the brain has experienced too much emotion, has become overwhelmed by feeling, so it numbs *all* feelings. I have met many clients with dissociative disorder who do not realize what is happening to them. They think they are losing their minds, but in fact they are experiencing an episode of disassociation, which leaves them feeling detached from the world around them.

It can be quite scary to experience it. I did, one evening when my father came flying through my bedroom door and screamed in my face. I remember thinking, *I'm not really here anyway so it doesn't matter*. That feeling of disassociation stayed with me for some time. In fact, it wasn't until I started to build a life and work my way out of that situation that it left me fully. But I can vividly remember it still, like a fog that wrapped itself about me so that nothing felt real and nothing could reach me.

—

CASE STUDY
The burden of secrets

One warm afternoon in May, I had a young teenage girl tell me in my clinic, 'I don't want to get my mother into trouble. What will happen if I tell you something bad?' I explained to her that depending on the severity of it, I might have to report it.

She really didn't want to divulge what was happening in her life, but the pressure and weight of the secret she was keeping had become too much, and she told me, 'My mother is an alcoholic. She sometimes collects me from school drunk. My friends' parents won't let them get a lift with me because they know she is drinking. She steals money from me. I hate living in this house. I don't know what to do.'

This young girl's life was in chaos, but she was also very loyal to her mother. Addiction was stealing her childhood. Her father had brought her to me because he was worried that she was suicidal. His concerns were warranted. She felt completely trapped and powerless. That is a very dangerous place for a child to find themselves in, because they don't have the cognitive ability at that young age to manage those feelings or to see that they will get out of that situation eventually.

When I spoke to the girl's father, I explained in very clear terms what I felt needed to happen to save his daughter and his family. Later that week, he rang me to inform me that his wife had gone into rehabilitation for her addiction. I met his daughter the following week and she was in better spirits, but she was nervous because this was her mother's second time going for help. Fortunately, after this second intervention, her mother did improve.

I later met her mother, and in our conversations she revealed that she had been sexually assaulted as a teenager. The trauma in her early life was causing chaos in her adult life. This chaos in her adult life was, in turn, causing trauma in her daughter's young life, which could easily become chaos in her daughter's adult life, and on and on the story goes.

—

The spiral of destruction caused by addiction can seem never-ending – unless you believe you have the power to disrupt it. It's a message that I am at pains to give to teenagers in my clinic who are dealing with the same issues that I faced in my young life, and who often feel trapped, without hope of escape. I say, 'I know it doesn't feel like this now, but you have a life waiting for you outside your family. Not long from now, you will go into that wonderful life and thrive. Think about that when you feel things are hopeless, because things are not hopeless, they're difficult at the moment, but they won't always be like that.' I say this to them because I know I needed to hear it when I was a teenager, but those words never came. And so I pass them on now, and every time I rejoice when I see the impact they have on the young person I'm chatting with.

The vicious circle of fear-based behaviour

This brings us back to positive feedback loops and familiar patterns of behaviour, whereby the thing you take into your life to make it better is the very thing that is causing your life to collapse. I certainly saw this in my life. My father used alcohol to manage his troubled feelings, but it caused his life to spiral into chaos, and it destroyed the relationship he had with his family. It's a vicious circle that so many people get trapped inside: troubling feelings/memories + substance (to quieten feelings) = chaos and dysfunction in life. And the circle keeps repeating.

But remember: you are only a prisoner to your patterns of behaviour for as long as you fail to see them. Your escape route is to become aware of what you do in response to not feeling good. As the child of an addict parent this can be very tricky. You can end up feeling that chaos is your comfort zone, which makes you seek it out, or create it if it's not there. This is very common for someone who experienced early childhood trauma. Living in constant tension becomes your reality, and without it you can feel lost, which can make you look to replicate it throughout your life, either by the person you choose as your partner or through maladaptive behaviours, such as sexual promiscuity, alcohol, drugs, obsessive or controlling actions.

The tension you experienced growing up in a dysfunctional environment changes how you perceive the world. Now, you view everything as a potential threat. I often use the image of your mind being like a sieve: it takes its shape during the formative years of childhood, through the early experiences you have, and then throughout adulthood positive or negative experiences either get through the sieve, or don't get through, depending on your particular experience growing up. So, if you experienced dysfunction or chaos in childhood, the sieve will only allow negative thoughts through. Anything that is good or wholesome gets caught in the sieve, like pasta, and cannot penetrate. This is how your perception gets changed.

The other common reaction is to feel deeply afraid of chaos and strive to keep it at bay. If this is your reaction to childhood trauma, you can become pathologically controlling of every little aspect of your life – and the lives of those you love. You are motivated by the fear of chaos, and all your energy – mental and emotional – is taken up trying to outsmart it and outrun it. Just like living in chaos, this rigid and futile adherence to no-chaos is also an exhausting way to live.

The long-lasting effects of family dysfunction

Growing up in a dysfunctional family unit can lead to many different issues in adult life.

Sibling conflict

Siblings often struggle to connect with one another. They can be very conflicted as they continue the dysfunction of their family unit into their adult lives. I have observed in my work how siblings often find it difficult to be around one another because they remind each other of the chaos they grew up in. So, they avoid each other.

If you have a conflicted relationship with your siblings, think about the dynamic of that conflict. Is it a consequence of your family of origin? What would it mean to you for that to be healed? What would need to happen to fix that relationship?

Control issues

As noted above, children who grow up in dysfunction can often become controlling adults as a backlash against the chaos they experienced in childhood. They make a promise to themselves that they will never live in that type of environment again. If they become too controlling, however, it can lead to their life spiralling out of control. This is one of the paradoxes of life, and I encounter it regularly. I've met so many men and women who work hard to control everything and then are completely confused as to how their life is spiralling out of control. They cannot fathom how the people in their life find it difficult to be around them because of the amount of control they need in order to feel safe. Again, the very thing they are struggling so hard to avoid is the very thing they are bringing into their life.

Replicating dysfunction

We often choose a partner who mirrors the behaviours of our early caregiver. This allows us to revisit the trauma of our childhood by bringing it into our adult life. If you notice that you have a tendency to do this, the more aware you become of it, the more likely it is that you will not unconsciously replicate the patterns of your childhood. It is vitally important that you think about the people you bring into your life and the benefit of them to your life.

Attachment issues

Research shows that when a child is unable to depend on their caregiver to help them regulate their emotions, the part of the brain that helps them make sense of their feelings doesn't develop properly. This stunted development can emerge as mental health issues in adolescence or adulthood.

One of the most painful experiences in adulthood – and one that can leave you feeling powerless – is the realization that you are replicating your early childhood experience with your own children. A negative early attachment can cause an adult to struggle to connect with their own children. I saw my own father become depressed when he started to see the relationship he had created with his children. I know when he started out as a parent, he hoped that it could heal the wrongs of his own childhood. But those aspirations faded incrementally as he became disillusioned with parenting. Alcohol destroyed whatever chance he had of fixing his life.

If only my father had understood how powerful those invisible forces are, and how negative brain chemistry can be reversed and healed. It requires dealing with those early experiences, becoming aware of the impact your family of origin had on your development, and avoiding negative behaviours that can disrupt your peace and happiness. If he had done that, his life would have been different. He would still have his family.

The familiarity of dysfunction

When you grow up with addiction in the family, it can have a profound impact on your life. Often, the partner we choose to enter into a relationship with as an adult allows us to continue the life we are used to. In my experience, people who have grown up with this type of dysfunctionality as children find peace and quiet difficult to manage. They are used to screaming, shouting and chaos, so sitting in silence can cause them to become agitated.

Clients will say to me, 'Sometimes, when things are going good, I decide to destroy that peace by doing something crazy.' I have heard this more times than I care to remember. But at the same time, they cannot understand why they crowbar their lives open with chaos. They beat themselves up for being so self-destructive, but it's deeper than that. It's the familiarity of dysfunction that they crave. Healthy, balanced relationships are terrifying and uncomfortable. The prolonged suffering that this type of mindset brings into their life is devastating. They often move into relationships with addictive or abusive people, because they are used to that type of life.

—

CASE STUDY
Living inside a damaging pattern

I had a client who used sex to manage her feelings. She struggled with intimacy and was aware that once she got close to someone, she pushed them away. But she didn't know why, and she also didn't really understand why she felt compelled to use dating apps for random sexual encounters.

I asked her to make a list of the things she did in response to feeling low, and also asked her to think about the attachment style she'd had with her primary caregiver. During this task, she disclosed that she had been sexually abused as a child by a neighbour. The fact that she was using dating apps to have sexual encounters with strangers was deeply confusing to her. She wondered whether the neighbour who had abused her had observed in her that she was curious about sex and potentially promiscuous. Victims of sexual predators often wrongly blame themselves.

In this case, the woman started to realize that her compulsive sexual behaviour was a response to her negative feelings and memories of being abused. She was ensuring that she experienced in adulthood the shame she had felt as a child. She was a victim of sexual abuse. Her abuser was dead and she had never disclosed to anyone what had happened to her. Her family and friends couldn't understand why she struggled in life. She was stuck in a very destructive positive feedback loop: the thing she was using to manage her trauma was the thing that retraumatized her. She told me, 'When I feel low, I just want to be used by people, at least that way I feel something, it's better than feeling nothing.'

The emotion in the room as she came to understand what she was doing to her life was incredible to witness. Later, she deleted the dating apps. She went back to them at times, but through awareness and effort she moved away from that behaviour. Eventually, she was able to conduct a loving relationship with someone she trusted.

She was resistant at first; she didn't want to lose that buzz she got when meeting a stranger. She felt alive, the thrill, the dopamine hit was all consuming. But the comedown afterwards – the shame, the guilt, the worry about STIs – it was all part of the cycle. We broke her habit by allowing her to see that anonymous sex wasn't actually all that exciting, and that she was losing a lot by giving herself away to people who didn't deserve to be with her. She started to value herself.

—

Trauma often presents like this. People think that self-harm is just cutting yourself, but people harm themselves in all kinds of different ways. When a person is victimized in childhood, they can victimize themselves in adulthood, to replicate those early feelings. It is familiar to them.

CASE STUDY
The alcoholic's child

I met a client a couple of years ago who I'll call Susan. She came to me because she felt her life had become stuck. It wasn't until the second session that she revealed she was living with addiction. The following exchanges are based on a number of sessions we had.

> SUSAN: I suppose I might as well just come out and tell you, I drink a lot.
>
> RICHARD: Thank you for telling me that. Was that hard to say?
>
> SUSAN: Yes, I've never really said it before. I mean, I've had partners who told me I drink too much, but I've never really said it, but I suppose if I'm going to get anything from these sessions, I might as well tell the truth.
>
> RICHARD: When you say a lot, do you mean you cannot stop?
>
> SUSAN: Yes, I guess so. I haven't not had a daily drink for years. Couldn't tell you when I last fell asleep without drink.
>
> RICHARD: Is it difficult to use the label 'alcoholic'?
>
> SUSAN: Yes, very.
>
> RICHARD: Why?
>
> SUSAN: Because alcoholics are losers.
>
> RICHARD: Are you an alcoholic?
>
> SUSAN: I guess so.
>
> RICHARD: Are you a loser?
>
> SUSAN: Must be.
>
> RICHARD: Can you have an issue with alcohol and not be a loser?
>
> SUSAN: I don't know. I feel like a loser.
>
> RICHARD: Is it that feeling of being a loser that motivates you to drink, or is it the other way around?
>
> SUSAN: I think drinking makes those feelings of being a loser go away.

RICHARD: Describe those feelings.

SUSAN: My life is shit, I live in this awful apartment, my
   boyfriend cheats on me and I still don't dump him,
   my job is pathetic, and I drink every night. That's a
   loser in my book.

RICHARD: Not in mine, but thank you for describing that
   for me. Have you always felt like this?

SUSAN: For as long as I can remember I have felt like a
   loser.

RICHARD: Can I ask about your parents? What was it like
   growing up in their relationship?

SUSAN: Oh God. I don't know if I want to get into all of
   this. It wasn't good.

RICHARD: What wasn't good about it?

SUSAN: Oh, everything. My father was your typical
   Irishman – work, the pub, dinner, fighting, repeat.

RICHARD: When you say fighting, do you mean with
   your mother?

SUSAN: Everyone. He's the most unhappy man I've
   known. I remember him throwing the Christmas
   dinner through the window because the gravy burnt
   his tongue. He had been drinking all morning and
   was very drunk by dinner.

RICHARD: I'm sorry to hear you had to experience that.
   How old were you?

SUSAN: I was about nine. He also fell into the Christmas
   tree and broke it. The neighbours were used to him
   and all the screaming that went on in our house.

RICHARD: Did you have siblings?

SUSAN: I had one older sister, Mary, she was much older. I
   think they tried to have a child after her but it didn't
   happen, and I was a surprise. Mary was twelve years
   older, so by the time I reached ten, she was gone. I
   was on my own with them. Nightmare, really.

RICHARD: Did Mary witness your dad's behaviour?

SUSAN: Not so much. It became worse when she left.
   That's the weird thing, she doesn't have the same

memories as I do. It really annoys me. But she got out early, I suppose.

RICHARD: Would you describe your childhood as dysfunctional?

SUSAN: Yes, it was. But I haven't really admitted it to myself. My father died two years ago now, and the way my mother talks about him drives me crazy. Like he was a saint.

RICHARD: What upsets you the most about how your mother talks about him?

SUSAN: It's that Irish thing of never speaking ill of the dead. She goes on about him like he was the greatest guy in the world. I want to scream from the top of my head, 'He was an abusive drunk!'

RICHARD: What stops you from saying it?

SUSAN: I play along with it all.

RICHARD: Why do you do that?

SUSAN: I don't want to upset my mother. He is dead now, so what good is that?

RICHARD: When we experience dysfunction in our formative years, it can change how we see the world, and we can seek out people who will replicate the environment we are familiar with. Does that sentence mean anything to you?

SUSAN: Too much. I always dated guys who were no good. Whenever I met someone who respected me and was decent, I ran a mile. I couldn't handle it.

RICHARD: What couldn't you handle?

SUSAN: Someone treating me well.

RICHARD: You don't deserve to be treated well?

SUSAN: I never thought so.

RICHARD: Or maybe it wasn't familiar to you?

SUSAN: Yeah, I think that's it, too.

RICHARD: Are you sitting here today because you realize you deserve better?

SUSAN: Yes. (*She is very upset.*)

That was the moment Susan's life began to change. She started to see herself differently. We all have that power.

—

One of the most liberating things you can do after growing up with addiction or dysfunction is to forgive the parent(s) who hurt you. It is helpful to be able to see your parents as individuals who were hurt before you arrived, and who didn't have the capacity to prevent it from tainting their lives. We are all the product of the family system we came up in, but we are not powerless to overcome those experiences. We can wallow in them and give away our agency, or we can become powerful and use those early negative experiences as motivation to thrive.

You have more power than you think. It can feel incredibly disempowering to get caught in a pattern of behaviour that you know is bad for you. Once you've realized this, don't expect change to happen immediately, expect to fall backwards a little. This is what causes most people to fail in their endeavours, such as trying to eat a healthier diet. They have one bad day, and they give up. Of course, bad days will come. If you expect them, they will not be such a surprise and won't have the power to undo all your efforts. Remember, you have been engaging in that pattern of behaviour for the majority of your life, so it's a strong habit. But the more you correct it when it comes back into your life, the more it will start to disappear.

We are not doomed to repeat behaviours that were modelled for us as children; they are powerful associations, yes, but we are also very powerful and we can move away from negative patterns of behaviour. We first have to understand what those patterns are, then intentionally disrupt them, and then make the effort to cultivate healthier behaviours and responses to stress. We all have the power to heal our relationships with ourselves and others.

What you can do
List one behaviour you would like to eradicate from your life. Write down what the behaviour is, and then write down how you would prefer to respond. Next, write down what might

get in the way of that new response happening. And finally, consider how you might react to any setbacks.

For example, let's say that you slam doors when you are stressed. Your list might look like this.

- I don't want to slam doors any more.
- I would like to just walk away when a situation becomes too heated.
- I think I've been doing it for so long, I might fall back on it.
- If I do, I won't just give up, I'll try to start again.

YOUR GENOGRAM

On your genogram, write in any addiction issues beside any family member, past or present, who experienced them. Can you see patterns emerging through the generations? Were these issues handed down from one person to the next?

Now, let's consider the pattern of behaviour when faced with stress.

1. How do your parents respond to stress? Write in their key coping reactions.
2. Write in your key coping reactions. Do you respond the same way as your parents?
3. How would you like to respond to stress? And how would you like your children to respond to stress?

12.   Separation and exclusion

A couple engaged in conflicted separation is a very difficult thing for everyone in the family unit to experience. It can leave residual bad feelings for years. It impacts on a child's reservoir of resilience and can leave lasting emotional scars from which some children never recover. Most couples want to separate in a healthy way, but that is not easy to achieve, because there are generally a lot of hurt feelings still simmering from the lead-up to the separation. In my experience, couples rarely separate because of a mutual desire to end the relationship. There is very often an injured party – one member of the relationship who is being left or has been hurt by the behaviour of the other partner.

I know this from first-hand experience, too. I remember standing at the bottom of the stairs while my mother threw my father out of the house. It was a terrible scene. One I rarely revisit in my mind. My grandmother is there, upset. My mother is telling him to get out, telling him how much hurt he has caused his family.

My father's response is to ask, 'What about me?'

Addiction, in my experience, impacts the addict's levels of empathy. They become so consumed in their own world of addiction, everyone else is a minor actor getting in the way of their activity. The family are nags, bringing the cold light of reality into their comfortably dark world.

'What about me?'

I have long wondered what my father meant by that. Perhaps, he was just thinking of himself, or perhaps he genuinely feared what would happen to him now that he was out of the house. He wasn't a very functioning individual. So, in some ways, I get what he meant. He didn't want to leave, because things were very comfortable for him. He had a wife who fed and looked after him, a family he could show off at public occasions, and a life of alcohol he didn't really have to be responsible for. The status quo suited him. But when he said those words – 'What about me?' – it enraged me, and I slammed the front door shut on him.

I have tried not to think too much about that moment, but that image of the door slamming shut is one that troubled me for a long time. For years afterwards, whenever I heard a door slam I'd think of that moment and it would crack the marrow of my soul. How we process our experiences and store them into memory is hugely significant. I was forced to confront adult themes at a young age and experienced the impact this has on well-being. Children don't want to think of their parents as sexual beings, and they certainly don't want to be involved in their sexual promiscuity. My discovery of my father's infidelity, and the subsequent fallout, damaged my well-being for some time. I became sullen and difficult to be around.

I have witnessed this many times in my clinic: children having to face adult themes, and the destruction it causes to the entire family. When children are used as allies by parents, it can damage them for life. Children do not have the ability to comprehend what is happening to them and their family. They often feel happy that the parent is confiding in them; they feel helpful and useful, but the damage can last a lifetime.

The curse of distrust

My father's affair, alcoholism and general bad behaviour forced him out of his loving family. Those early days of separation were very difficult to experience. I found that, nearly, the hardest part. I was embarrassed that my parents had separated. It was shameful. When my friends' parents mentioned my father, I had to hide my anger and resentment. Helping my mother through those early days of separation was tough. We were great friends. It was the three of us for a long time: my grandmother, mother and myself. She worked hard to rebuild her life, and slowly she managed it. It was incredible to watch. The strength and perseverance she displayed was inspiring. I was there alongside my grandmother, supporting her, too.

But in truth, I was all over the place. I was closed off from people. Having watched the awful scenes that played out between my parents before and during the separation, and having witnessed my father walking away from us – a loss that he could have avoided by making different choices – I developed an unshakeable belief that people let you down. As a result, I stopped trusting people. I started expecting the worst from everyone. My mother's thinking changed, too. I'd hear her say, 'He gave her a terrible time, he was a drunk and abusive. You know, the usual.' I used to point out that I didn't think that was the usual. It is one of the most commonly used protective interventions: expect the worst, so you are not let down when it happens. If you are happy, enjoying life and expecting the best to happen, you will get some land when something terrible inevitably befalls you.

I have met this logic many times in my clinic, as people try to ensure they never feel hurt. But the reality is that you are constantly hurting yourself with this logic. You never trust anyone, you don't let people get to know you, you become deceptive with your feelings, even deceptive with your behaviour. That is such an unhealthy frame of mind.

The girlfriend I was with at the time broke off the relationship, thus confirming my bias: people will let you down. Of course, looking at it now, I know I was not an easy person to be with. I pushed her away, to see if she would stay. This is something people often do to ascertain if they are in a safe environment. She was a beautiful person, we were great friends, but the chaos I had lived in massively impacted my ability to be joyful in those early years of my twenties. I didn't enjoy my own company in those days, not to mention someone else enjoying being with me. I was suspicious of people, expecting the worst, ready to fight if someone said something to annoy me, aggressive and closed-minded. The opposite of who I am today. That was the impact familial separation had on me. It changed my personality for a while.

I have seen this in my clinic: children closed off and guarded about their feelings. They think they are protecting themselves by erecting an invisible guard around them. I can see through it. They think it is an impenetrable wall, but with a few questions I'm allowed in and they show themselves to be honest, vulnerable and strong. Children generally do not have sophisticated coping mechanisms – nor do adults, for that matter. Closing themselves off is the best way they can think of to protect against the perceived threat. Teenage boys are particularly adept at this intervention. But it's an illusion of safety, nothing more.

Feeling responsible

'I hope you are happy.'

Five little words that have gone around in my mind for over twenty years. My father went to collect my mother at the train station one afternoon. She had spent the weekend with my eldest brother and he had informed her of our father's affair, after I had told him about it. When she arrived into Cork station, she confronted him with the information. Of course, he denied it. But his web of lies had trapped him. It was over.

He rang me. 'I hope you are happy,' is what he said, and then hung up.

I immediately thought he was going to kill himself and that it would be on me. I fell back on the stairs, my head in my hands. How could I go on if my father killed himself because I had exposed his affair? I didn't know what to do. I felt responsible for so much at that time. I felt responsible for my mother's pain, and for the atmosphere that existed in the family after that moment. I thought perhaps I shouldn't have said anything and just got on with it. I felt weak for telling my siblings. I could see my grandmother's upset; she loved my father. Now she had to watch her daughter manage the separation from him. And all because I couldn't keep it to myself. Those days were some of the hardest I have experienced. I felt numb for a long time after that. And I have seen what it does to children in my clinic. It engenders terribly destructive feelings of shame, blame and guilt. I lived with those feelings for a long time, carried them around like a dark shadow. Those feelings caused me a considerable amount of trouble.

One morning, my mother dropped me to college. The drive in

was awful. She was upset and unsure how she would manage caring for her mother with so little funds coming into the house, now that my father was gone.

I remember sitting in a lecture theatre in UCC when I suddenly felt like I was going to pass out. It felt like I was going to have a heart attack. I didn't know what to do. I got up and left the lecture and went to hospital, presenting myself at A&E. The doctors checked me over and once they realized what was happening, they asked me if I had any stress in my life. They gently explained that I had just experienced a panic attack.

I had a lot of stress in those early days of my parents' separation. More than I wanted to admit. I felt responsible for the separation, I felt responsible for my mother's struggle, my grandmother's upset and my father's uncertain future. I felt responsible for all of it. But I didn't tell anyone how I was feeling. Young men are very bad at expressing what is going on in their internal world. They view it as a weakness. I have worked with so many young men struggling to articulate their thoughts and feelings. The idea that emotions are a sign of weakness, and boys shouldn't express them, has caused a lot of suffering for men, in particular. It certainly did for me.

Parental alienation

Separation is one of the most difficult experiences a family can go through. When someone close to us dies, we go through the natural grieving process, supported by friends and neighbours. But when a couple separates, lines are drawn and sides are taken. There might be very little support – and those who offer it will also be forced to choose a side. The breakdown of the family can cause a different type of grief, a far more pervasive and complicated grief that can impact all facets of your life.

When an injured party feels powerless, they can use the children as proxies in the post-separation battleground. I have worked with so many families where this has happened, and the devastation visited on each member of the family is absolute. When a parent (usually the primary caregiver) uses their power of influence over their children to turn them against the other parent, it results in a process called 'parental alienation'. Children are the biggest losers in this process. There is nothing more catastrophic for a child's psychological well-being than to be forced to make false allegations against a loving parent.

In my experience, parents who use their children in this way eventually become alienated from their children as they grow older and become more sophisticated in their analysis of what happened. If they come to understand that they were used by their parent in the most profoundly manipulative way, they start to pull away from that parent. If they are faced with the realization that they were coerced into saying something terrible about a parent, it is deeply upsetting. No child wants to think that a parent could put their own interests before the needs of their children, and use them to cause maximum damage to the partner they are in a conflict with. But parents are people, and people can do terrible things when they are hurt. As the old saying goes: hurt people, hurt people.

A parent who does this has very low levels of maturity and will, at times, display high levels of narcissism and low differentiation of self. This concept of differentiation of self was identified by psychiatrist and researcher Dr Murray Bowen in the 1970s to describe the ability to distinguish between thoughts and feelings in an emotional relationship system. If a parent has a low differentiation of self, the parent's and child's feelings become tangled together, they become enmeshed.

If your parent has a low differentiation of self, they see you, their child, as an extension of themselves, so their hurt is your hurt, and getting you to say terrible things or to reject your other loving parent is fair game because, in their eyes, you have both been so badly hurt and let down by that parent.

A child who experiences this kind of relationship with their parent can often find it difficult to articulate their own feelings. They are not sure how they feel, because their feelings have always been their parent's feelings. The complicity of those feelings shared by parent and child can be very rewarding for the child, as they feel at one with their primary caregiver. Remember what I said about attachment: everything in early life is about survival. Expressing the parent's feelings can ensure the safety and security of the child in that relationship. While it can bind the primary caregiver and the child, it can cause irreparable damage to the parent being rejected.

The experience of being rejected by their child or children can devastate the parent. This is certainly the case if there are false allegations involved. This can quickly cause the parent's friendship group to shrink, as people do not want to be associated with someone who would do whatever was alleged by the children. The financial cost of fighting in the courts for contact with their children is ruinous; the emotional cost, indeed the physical cost, is so great that the rejected parent has no choice but to surrender to their children's wishes – which are really the wishes of the primary caregiver – and stop asking to see them. Of all the different phenomenon I have worked with as a systemic family psychotherapist this is by far the most catastrophic for the family unit. I have described this process as 'scorched earth'. Nothing good is left.

If your parents separated and this description is making sense to you, it is important that you go to see someone professionally to work out that experience. No child should be used like this, but unfortunately it happens far more than we would like to admit. Reconnecting with your parent who was rejected could be one of the most healing, restorative experiences in your life. If you said something about your parent that you now regret or know to be false, you must forgive yourself. You were a child, and everything in your world was designed to keep you close to your primary caregiver. It is not your fault if you said something you now wish you hadn't about your mother or father. Talk to someone, be compassionate towards yourself, and see the person who orchestrated this as vulnerable and unable to manage their deep feelings of hurt. It's now time to move forward and thrive.

Normative estrangement

My own relationship with my father was estranged, not because my mother turned me against him but because I decided he was too much of a negative influence in my life at that time. That is called 'normative estrangement'. Children often reject a parent who they feel is not healthy to be around. The difference between this and parental alienation is that with parental alienation, children are led to reject a loving parent without any real cause or reason. Normative estrangement, on the other hand, is a personal choice made by the child, based on their lived experience of that parent. It is deliberate and comes from the child themself.

Children can often feel guilty or responsible for a parent's unhappiness when they have decided to stop seeing them for a period of time. It is an innate instinct to love your parent. But sometimes the relationship is not healthy and you need some time to grow, free from their influence. When my father left my orbit, life started to change dramatically for me. I wasn't the 'dark poet' he had described, I was a young man learning how to find my way in life, free from his negative influence.

It takes a lot of strength to make that choice, and we often struggle with it, but sometimes it is necessary for our development.

YOUR GENOGRAM

1. In your genogram, record any separation or split in the family.
2. Write out why you believe the split occurred, and your reaction to it.

In light of what you have learned from this chapter, have you changed your thinking about someone from whom you are estranged? As you see it now, what was the reason for that relationship ending? What would you need to do to heal that separation?

Are you a child of parental alienation? Would you like to heal that? If so, how could you reconnect with the person who is estranged from you?

PART SIX

Navigating Love

WHEN I WAS A TEENAGER, I LOVED MUSIC. I PLAYED THE GUITAR and fancied myself as the next John Lennon. Minus the incredible voice and penetratingly innovative lyrics. I played in a band and gigged around Cork in the mid-1990s. One evening, when I came home early from a gig, everything changed.

The house was empty, or so I thought. The phone rang, and it was answered before I got to it. We had two phones in the house and the other was next to my father's bed. I went upstairs. The yellow moon in the side window of the house. I remember that so clearly, because I saw my shadow climbing the stairhead. It all looked so surreal – the letter box rattling with the north Atlantic wind behind me, the moon on my shoulder. This moment became another one of those I would replay, over and over again, as I moved into adulthood.

I listened outside my parents' bedroom as my father talked, in a hushed, drunk voice that was close to shouting, to a woman who wasn't my mother. From the content of the conversation it was pretty clear they were having an affair. The revelation of an affair didn't really come as a shock to me. I had suspected that my father was messing around. In fact, the affair wasn't the worst of his behaviour. If he had been a decent person, the affair wouldn't have sullied our relationship massively. I mean, it would have caused problems, the fact that he was cheating on my mother, but it wouldn't have destroyed my relationship with him completely. I could understand, even at that young age, that his relationship with my mother was separate from his relationship with his children. But the fact he was so difficult to live with, he ruled over the house with an iron fist, and now he had betrayed all of us with this latest tryst, that was all a bit too much to take. There had been clues: nights he didn't come home, marks on his face like he had been attacked, random gifts he received and when I asked about them his answers differed, depending on his sobriety. But this night, as I stood trembling outside his bedroom, my suspicions were confirmed.

I really didn't know what to do with that information. My immediate response was to go downstairs and smoke my mother's Consulate cigarettes. As I sat there, flicking the ash into the fire, I wondered what to do. Should I tell my mother? What would that mean for us, as a family? My father was a difficult man, to say the least, but would I be happy if he left? Would he leave? It was far too much for my teenage mind to comprehend. So, I just held on to it for a while – until it became intolerable, and then I told my brother.

We decided to confront our father and ask him to tell our mother what he was up to. Of course, it didn't go well. My father denied the affair, scrambled around for excuses, but in the end told us that if we wanted to tell our mother lies, we could. Honourable stuff. And that was that. But that event impacted me massively. It destroyed the relationship I was in with my girlfriend. I became very insecure about infidelity, believing that everyone would hurt me, cheat on me and leave me. I was despairing and not pleasant to be around. That's what happens to children when they experience traumatic events in their formative years. The inner voice changes and becomes more negative. Mine certainly did.

When I look back now, I can see the hurt young boy who struggled to comprehend the pressures his family life placed on him. The boy desperately trying to protect himself in a very difficult environment, using maladaptive interventions to keep himself safe. The young boy who thought he could manage it all, but it placed incredible strain on his well-being.

It wasn't until a few months later, when my eldest brother told my mother what was happening, that things came to the terrible conclusion I described in Chapter 12. After my mother had confronted him at the train station with this information, my father rang me and left me with the words, 'I hope you are happy.' I collapsed on the foot of the stairs, thinking his suicide would be my fault. I struggled after that for a while. I carried his parting words around in my head for years. Like all the rest, it went around in a loop. Playing on shuffle. Impacting my joy and sense of self, and my own ability to give and experience love.

My father's inability to love us – at least in the ways we needed – took root in me as an inability to love myself or feel loved by others. It was a generational pattern being handed down to me, and it would take a long time for me to be able to see that and finally be able to give and experience love fully.

13. *The language of love*

The concept that different languages may develop different cognitive skills reaches back centuries. American linguists Edward Sapir and Benjamin Lee Whorf put forward the idea in the 1930s that speakers of different languages might view the world differently due to the rules and constraints of that language. This theory has been going in and out of style for many years. Lera Boroditsky explains: 'Around the world people communicate with one another using a dazzling array of languages – 7,000 or so all told – and each language requires very different things from its speakers. For example, suppose I want to tell you that I saw Uncle Vanya on 42nd Street. In Mian, a language spoken in Papua New Guinea, the verb I used would reveal whether the event happened just now, yesterday or in the distant past, whereas in Indonesian, the verb wouldn't even give away whether it had already happened or was still coming up. In Russian, the verb would reveal my gender.'

Therefore, how we think is directly linked to the language we speak, its rules and suppositions. This is known as the principle of linguistic relativity. This principle states that the way people think of the world is influenced directly by the language they use to talk about it. Some argue that people can only perceive aspects of the world for which their language has words. But in practice, languages don't limit our ability to perceive the world or to think about the world, rather they focus our attention and thought on specific aspects of the world.

Speaking of positivity

When we start to think more positively and optimistically, our language changes and with it changes our perception of the world. The more positive the language we use to describe our experiences, the more we begin to thrive. People who are depressed use negative language to describe their life. Listen to the internal language you speak: is it positive? If you notice that it is often negative, start reframing the events you encounter using more positive language.

—

CASE STUDY
Self-love through self-talk

I had a client tell me that he felt his life had dramatically changed when he became more aware of why he framed his lived experiences in negative language. He said that his dad had always let him down. His parents separated when he was young and he couldn't depend on his father. He described birthday parties where his father hadn't turned up, afternoons sitting on the stairs waiting for his father to collect him, but he never showed. He said he remembered saying to himself when he was about eight years old, 'Stop expecting something good to happen.' This intervention was significant for this child because it protected him from being hurt. But now, at thirty years old, it was making his life a misery. He was filtering every life experience through this negative lens, and it was causing huge suffering.

He started to dismantle this negativity, by being more intentional about how he wanted to talk to himself. He didn't suppress that early voice, but when he heard it popping up, he simply spoke more positively to himself about his life. He made a list of things he would like to say about himself and started to introduce them into his thinking. As his internal language became more positive, his entire demeanour started to change.

When I saw him first, he was hunched over on the seat, shoulders slouched and head down, almost apologetic for the person he was. As he began to speak a more positive language, his body language also changed.

—

If our inner voice is hard and critical and negative, it colours everything. But if we speak to ourselves with love, that is a powerful expression of self-care and nurturing. We all have that power. We can all be more positive in how we talk to ourselves.

I think, as Irish people, we can almost be embarrassed to say we love ourselves. This is something I say to students all the time: 'It wouldn't just be nice to love yourself, it is necessary for a happy life.'

What you can do
Think about the adjectives you use to describe your experiences. Are they positive descriptive words? Make a list of them.

If you notice that there are more negative adjectives than positive, make an alternative list of positive adjectives and start to intentionally use them to describe your daily experiences.

Your love language

A love language is how we experience and express love, and we each speak a different love language. This again comes back to what you experienced in your early years and to your initial sense of security in your early attachment to your primary caregiver. Whether that was secure, insecure, avoidant or ambivalent, it will directly impact how you experience love and, very importantly, how you express love.

I have on many occasions sat down with a couple in my clinic and listened as they described the differences between them. Often, they both describe feeling isolated in the relationship. I have been so struck by this deep sense of loneliness experienced by couples. I have listened to so many women relating the same story of isolation, poor or no communication, not feeling wanted, feeling unappreciated, undesired and exhausted with all the effort they have to make to keep their relationship moving forward. When I speak with the husband, there is a real sense of confusion, almost despair, as he articulates the inner turmoil of not knowing how to meet the needs of his wife. They are each speaking a different love language, one that was quite fluent in the early days but that has become incomprehensible over time.

One woman told me that she was drawn to her husband's silence and inner strength at the outset, only for that to become the source of her isolation and loneliness. His love language did not match hers and it had created a gulf between them. I see this very regularly.

It is important to become aware of the love language we speak, and why we speak it, because we need to become more fluent in each other's language if we want our relationships to flourish. The concept of love languages was developed by Gary Chapman in the early 1990s. He outlined five different love languages:

1. words of affirmation
2. physical touch
3. giving and receiving gifts
4. quality time
5. acts of service.

Think about your attachment style: how did it shape the love language you speak and feel? Think about your partner: do you both speak the same love language? Our early attachments inform how we experience and show love.

I often meet couples who are struggling to communicate love effectively to each other. One partner might say, 'I'm very affectionate and like to be touched and caressed,' while the other partner might not be very interested in that connection. A child who experienced an avoidant attachment style might struggle to connect emotionally with a partner as an adult. Everything in their early life told them: you must rely on yourself to satisfy your needs, nobody will do it for you. They might therefore experience love through acts of service, and struggle to communicate love through quality time, words of affirmation and physical touch. A person who experienced an anxious attachment style might feel loved through words of affirmation, gifts and physical touch. A person who experienced a secure attachment style might struggle to meet the needs of a partner with an anxious attachment style, because they feel they can never satisfy the needs of that partner.

Our attachment styles are the fundamental building blocks of how we express and receive love.

CASE STUDY
'I don't know how to love her'

I worked with a couple where the husband was neurodivergent and strug-gled with interpersonal relationships. His wife's love language was very clearly physical touch and words of affirmation; he was particularly low in this area. This had brought a significant amount of conflict into their lives.

In our first conversation, his wife expressed a sense of feeling unwanted, not desired. She said, turning to her husband, 'It would be nice, just once, to come down the stairs and have you tell me I look gorgeous when we're heading out for a night.'

Her husband sat there, silent, as she described life with him.

'We have talked about this a lot. Just yesterday we had a huge fight, he said that we would go for a walk when he came home from work, but I could tell he didn't want to. He lit the fire when he came in and was read-ing on his own. That wouldn't be so bad, but we had talked about being intimate early that morning, but he came into the bedroom dressed for work and just kissed my forehead and left. I don't know why I bother, it's just constant rejection.'

When I asked him to describe his experience of these events, he said, 'I'm a lecturer, so I talk all day; when I come home I don't really have the headspace for all the conversation, and Sinéad doesn't really want to hear about my day. We had talked about maybe being intimate that morning, but I woke up late and had to rush to get out, there was no time, and I didn't really feel like it. That's all. I love Sinéad, but I don't know *how* to love Sinéad any more. I feel like everything I do annoys her.'

This was the first time Sinéad had heard her husband express his feel-ings of inadequacy in relation to loving her. We explored their love languages. Sinéad was tactile and words of affirmation were important to her, while Garry experienced love in a more intellectual way. He felt loved when Sinéad valued his intelligence and engaged in thoughtful conversa-tion. He felt loved when she appreciated what he did around the house. They both spoke different love languages.

Garry said that he admired his wife but felt shame that he was causing her such pain. Sinéad broke down; she hadn't realized her husband strug-gled internally with their relationship and had felt that he was simply 'not interested in [me] any longer'. Their relationship had come to an impasse because they struggled to understand how each other expressed and felt love.

Those conversations were a breakthrough for them because they forged an understanding that had eluded them for so long. Once they knew they were loved, they were able to then work on *how* they loved each other. They both became more intentional and, over time, fluent in each other's love language.

—

Your love style

From the five love languages come the seven love styles. The combination of your attachment style and your communication style determine your love style. This refers to the manner in which you prefer to connect with romantic partners.

1. Appreciation

This love style is all about feeling loved through compliments and being praised. You feel valued when your partner articulates their appreciation for who you are and what you do in the relationship. I have had many women tell me, 'I would give anything just to hear him say how much he appreciates what I do to keep the whole family going.'

2. Activity

You feel loved and valued when your partner takes an interest in your hobbies and makes an effort to enjoy activities together.

3. Emotional

You feel loved when your partner is able to connect with you and support you through vulnerable emotions during emotionally challenging or difficult times.

4. Financial

You feel loved and valued when your partner is generous. It isn't about massive gifts but rather it's about feeling a treat or surprise was planned just for you – to give you joy.

5. Intellectual

You connect through the mind and feel loved when your partner values your intelligence, respects your opinion and takes part in thoughtful discussion of important issues. I have heard many clients express an incompatibility in this love language.

6. Physical

You crave physical love and feel cared for and supported when being touched and held by your partner. Physical intimacy is vitally important for your sense of being wanted and loved. This is not just about sex but about true intimacy, holding hands, hugging, embracing and feeling physically connected to each other. Of all the languages, in my experience this is the one that most couples struggle to speak to each other. The busyness of life, regular routine, banal chores, exhaustion after a long day, all impact the ability to connect physically. I have heard countless couples utter the same sentiment: after a long day, finally getting the kids to sleep, all they want is to relax without any conflict, so they avoid each other. Lack of physical intimacy can happen so easily, and you have to work to prevent this from creeping into your relationship. It can build up incrementally so that we don't realize it until the space between us is too great. Communication is key to preventing this from happening.

7. Practical

You feel special and valued when your partner takes care of the chores and offers practical help to lighten the daily load. This is not just about doing the necessary chores but about doing things that are unexpected and specifically for the benefit of the house and their partner. The lack of equity around household chores causes huge problems for couples.

What you can do

Here are some questions to help you identify your love language and style.

- When do you feel most loved by your partner?
- What are they doing in that moment?
- How do you show your partner that you love them?
- How do they let you know that they have felt your love?

Now think about these questions.

- What was your early attachment? That should now be clearly outlined in your genogram.
- What have you identified as your particular love language? Why is that your language? Think about how your parents expressed love to each other and to you – has that had an impact on how you experience and show love to your partner and family?
- What is your partner's love language? Do you both speak a different language?
- What would need to happen for you and your partner to become more fluent in each other's love language?

The key thing to remember is that you do not have to speak the same love language to have a deep, meaningful relationship. You have to become aware of each other's language and work to fulfil that for each other. Once you become aware of how to give and receive each other's love, you can learn to speak each other's love language.

YOUR GENOGRAM

You have compiled your own genogram – and it should be getting quite full by now. It's time to do the same for your partner. Prepare it in the same way, as best you can, going back to their grandparents and filling in as much as you know about each person's life. If your partner is willing to do this with you, it will be a good exercise to carry out together.

1. Fill in the love language of your parents on both genograms – what you both perceived growing up.
2. Now fill in each of your love languages. Is your partner's the same as yours? If not, is that causing issues between you?
3. What could you do to become more fluent in each other's language?
4. If you wanted your partner to become more aware of how you experience and give love, what would you need to say to them? What would they need to say to you in return?

14. The language of conflict

We all argue from time to time, that's a normal part of any close relationship. But how we were reared in those early years of our formation equips us with the tools to solve arguments in a respectful and heathy way, or in a disrespectful and damaging way. When our cognition becomes hot and we respond emotionally to a problem, how do we act?

I meet this regularly in couples therapy, where both members of the couple have been given very different tools to solve conflict. The following case study illustrates this very well.

—

CASE STUDY
Marital strife

Jane and Brian came to see me because they were worried that their fighting had escalated, and recently Jane had hit Brian. They had two children and were concerned about the impact their fighting was having on their children. Their eldest child had told a teacher about the fighting at home and this had been disclosed to Tusla – Child and Family Agency. This couple urgently needed a solution that would allow them to argue better and resolve issues effectively.

The following interactions are taken from a number of sessions I had with the couple.

> RICHARD: Can I ask you, Brian, to describe why you
> think we are here today?
> BRIAN: Well, I think we are here because things have
> to change, I'm not willing to live with things as
> they are any more. I can't go on with the way
> things are in the family, it's not fair on the children.
> [*Brian is upset now and crying.*] I feel like I've lost
> my family.

RICHARD: Thank you, Brian. Can I ask you the same question, Jane?

JANE: I feel the same. Things are not good at the moment, and if we were being honest, they probably haven't been good for a couple of years. Brian finds it hard to open up about things. When he comes home from work he doesn't want to talk; that makes me feel distant from him. He goes out for long cycles and I feel like he has no interest in me. I couldn't tell you the last time he organized something for us. I have to drive everything, and it's exhausting.

RICHARD: Can I ask you both about how you resolve conflict?

BRIAN: I think that is part of the issue. We don't.

JANE: Yeah, I'd agree that's a bit of the issue alright, we don't resolve it. Brian likes to just forget about it, but I like to try and work it out.

BRIAN: Well, your idea of working it out is shouting at me and expecting me to stand there and take it.

JANE: It's so hard to get a response from you, it drives me crazy. I'm so frustrated, I explode.

RICHARD: Can I ask you, Brian, how did your parents resolve conflict?

JANE: They didn't, very cold people.

RICHARD: Thank you, Jane. I'm going to ask you to listen to Brian as if he is someone else's husband. Please don't interrupt him, and I'll ask Brian to do the same when it's your turn.

JANE: Fine.

BRIAN: Jane isn't wrong. They were good country people. There wasn't a lot of talk about feelings or anything like that in the family. My parents wouldn't really argue, but you could tell when they were arguing. Dad would ask me to ask [Mother] something. There would often be long bouts of silence and no communication between them. That was hard as the eldest son. I was often the buffer between them. But never any shouting or hitting.

RICHARD: During those long silences, what was it like to live in the house?

BRIAN: Ah, grand really, I spent most of my time in my bedroom. I think I developed my love of my own space then. I'd spend hours studying chess books and chess moves. I don't remember being particularly sad. It wasn't very happy either.

RICHARD: What did you learn about how you resolve conflict from your parents?

BRIAN: I'd say what I learned is that conflict resolves itself, it just kind of resolves naturally. My dad wasn't a talker, he didn't say much, and my mother didn't tell you she loved you but she was always there, waiting for us after school and lunches packed. You felt loved but we didn't say it. I don't think I ever heard my parents tell me they loved me. But you knew you were, if that makes sense. So I don't say I love Jane that much either. But I do.

RICHARD: Can I ask you the same question, Jane, how did your parents resolve conflict?

JANE: Very differently to that. My father had a terrible temper. He could lose it easily, and my mother would shout at him, sometimes goading him to lose it, it wasn't nice to watch. But then they'd be fine again and they'd be all over each other.

RICHARD: Was that hard for you to witness?

JANE: Yeah, it was, but we were kids and we didn't know any different.

RICHARD: How did they resolve those conflicts?

JANE: Oh, there'd be shouting and door slamming, my mother would say something terrible about him, she'd threaten to leave him, or tell him to get out. He might leave and the next morning everything was fine again.

RICHARD: What do you think you learned about how conflict resolves?

JANE: Bit like Brian there, it just does. Words don't mean anything and sometimes we say terrible things in the heat of the moment, but it doesn't mean anything. Not everything has to have great meaning.

RICHARD: Is that where you think you differ?

JANE: Definitely. Brian takes everything to heart. I know I shouldn't say some of the things that I say, but it's in an argument. People say things that they don't mean. Myself and my sisters used to say terrible things to each other, but we're still friends. Well, I don't talk to one of them because she's got issues, I just avoid her.

RICHARD: I'm sorry to hear you have conflict with your sibling.

JANE: It's more complicated than that. She has moved back in with my parents and my mother gives her all her attention. She has a child and my mother has no time for our children because she has her hands full with her child. So that causes tension. But my mother always took sides. And she never took mine. I never felt respected or validated.

RICHARD: How did you get heard in that family dynamic?

JANE: I didn't.

RICHARD: When Brian doesn't argue back with you, do you feel that maybe some of that experience is coming up for you?

JANE: Oh definitely. It's really awful to have a partner who doesn't acknowledge you. I never felt acknowledged in my family, the eldest was the apple of their eye. They loved him. I was never seen. It was awful. I've done therapy trying to make sense of all that crap.

RICHARD: It sounds like a difficult environment for you to grow up in. How do you think Brian could acknowledge you?

JANE: Just say something. I'm saying awful things to him and he is just looking at me, it makes me worse. If he

just said something, told me to piss off, at least I'd feel
that I'm talking to someone.

RICHARD: Can I ask you some of the things you say in
the heat of an argument?

JANE: I hate him, how much of a disappointment he
is, I want a divorce, I married a robot. It's awful,
I know.

RICHARD: Where are the kids when this is happening?

JANE: They're upstairs.

RICHARD: Brian, what are you doing when Jane is saying
this?

BRIAN: I'm thinking about how to get out of this
relationship without damaging the kids.

RICHARD: What do you say in response to Jane's words?

BRIAN: Nothing. It feels unsafe, she has hit me and
thrown things at me. She broke our wedding photo
frame recently. It's getting worse.

RICHARD: Would you agree it's unsafe, Jane?

JANE: I don't think I would ever hurt Brian, but it has
been bad. I'm so frustrated, I don't know what to do.

I asked them to make a list of the negative legacies from their own
parents that they felt were impacting their relationship. We drafted a
contract that removed screaming, slamming doors and silences from
conflict. Slowly, we began to take the old negative habits out of their
interactions. At times, they would report that they had fallen back into
the old habits, but over the sessions those lapses became more and more
infrequent.

—

We are all driven by these invisible forces that can disrupt our happy
home. But once we become more aware of how we were raised,
and what we learned in those early years of our development and
maturation, we can start to critically evaluate whether some of
those beliefs, values and behaviours are good for us, or not. We can
begin to evaluate whether or not they push us forward in a positive
way to becoming who we want to be.

What you can do

Make a list of some of the positive and negative behaviours you think you assimilated during childhood – the legacy that is still being played out in your adult life. Now, make a list of your partner's. Compare them. Choose one you think is significant and needs to change.

Sit down with your partner and read your lists together. Ask which behaviours your partner thinks are significant and are impacting your relationship. Ask which one they think you both need to work on. Does it match yours? Now start the process of changing it.

Let's say you are like Jane and Brian, and there are high levels of conflict. Start by picking one aspect of your response during arguments, and change it. For example, you could say, 'Let's just agree when there is conflict we are not going to call each other names and use expletives to provoke each other.' Understanding why you do that, and where you learned it, is important, but the real work is in disrupting old habits with more positive behaviours.

Don't try to change the entire relationship in one go. Slowly remove aspects you know are destructive and unhelpful. If you try to fix everything at once, your attempt will only fail and make you feel powerless.

Remember, too much change is too much. Changing relational dynamics takes time, and at times you will fall back into old habits. When you are moving away from negative behaviours, expect a certain amount of failure as you move forward. If you expect things to change without any steps backwards, you will become dejected the moment you retreat into old learned behaviours. They are powerful and take time to weed out of your life.

YOUR GENOGRAM

It's important that you can see your response to conflict clearly.

1. Write down on the genogram your parents' styles of argument and conflict resolution. If you have the information, write that in for your grandparents as well. Think about your siblings and write in their styles, too. This will show you the patterns that are at work through the generations.

2. On your own genogram, write down the key ways you respond to conflict – or if you go to great lengths to avoid it. If you have a partner, add this information to their genogram. Can you see how your arguments are being shaped by those invisible forces laid down in your childhoods?

3. Identify any reactions you feel are unhelpful and that don't help to resolve conflict. Be honest. Make a contract with yourself that when conflict occurs, you won't reach for those familiar reactions.

4. Write a list of the reactions you would prefer to reach for, and make an intentional effort to use those in any argument from now on.

PART SEVEN

Choosing New Legacies as a Parent

MY FATHER USED TO SPEAK ABOUT HIS AWFUL CHILDHOOD. HIS mother played the children against each other and had favourites, while his father was ineffectual and weak. He certainly felt victimized by this family dynamic. No one encouraged him, no one saw his talent. His relationship with his mother was particularly fractured and problematic, so much so that it seeped into our relationship with her. Before we visited her, he would recount many awful moments when she had treated him badly. We would all feel sorry for him, which gave him a wonderful excuse for when he didn't live up to his responsibilities as a father and husband. How could he be accountable? He was a victim in his childhood. This mentality destroyed his promising career and life. Everyone owed him something. I used to listen as he roared down the phone at his boss in Dublin. The editor had the cheek to ask him to meet a deadline, or to give in his copy for the following day's article sober. As far as I could see, it shrank his life down, until he had nothing left. Only self-pity. He was victimized by his parents, his work, and eventually his family rejected him.

I clearly remember shocking him one evening as he grabbed me by the arm and tried to drag me down the stairs. He was outraged that I had turned my back on him and walked away in the middle of one of his drunken tirades. As he tried to drag me down the stairs, I looked at him and said, 'You always go on about how terrible life was for you as a child with your parents, but I never remember you saying anything about your dad dragging you down the stairs drunk and physically trying to harm you.' That stopped him dead in his drunken tracks. As I walked away, I shot back, 'And I won't be using this moment as an excuse later, when I'm a father, to hurt my children.'

I was sixteen years of age then, and I don't know if I fully understood what I was saying. But as I look at those words now, a father to three daughters, there was a lot of depth in what I said as a young teenager. And the reason he stopped dead was because I had brought him into contact with the lie he had been telling himself all his life.

When my children ask me about their grandfather they don't know, I explain he is a complicated guy who has good points and some bad points, like us all. The easiest thing would be to use those difficult moments from my childhood as an excuse for falling short as a father, a husband and a man. It would also be the most destructive thing I could do for my life. I know I'm not a victim. Those moments from my childhood motivate me in a very positive way. I promised myself I would never carry that forward in my life as a parent, that my children would never feel intimidated in my presence. My heart used to sink when I'd see his car was outside the house. I made a promise to myself many years ago that my children would never feel that. And no barman would know my name!

That young boy is in me still but, crucially, I have not let him become a negative force. I have worked to turn his experiences into powerful motivators for my present and future life. The boy inside my father allowed him to behave badly, to be a poor version of himself. It doesn't have to be like that. The boy inside me helps me to be a better father, a better husband and a better man. My father's legacy will not be my legacy.

15. Positive relations

Most of us are unaware of the complicated legacies that are handed down to us through the generations. If I asked you to think about your great-grandparents and their style of parenting and love language, would you know? Doubtful. But nonetheless we do receive legacies, good and bad, transmitted through the generations. Some are assimilated into new family legacies, while others never get passed on. My children will never know what it is like to live with an addicted parent. I know that experience, but it will end with me. We all have the power to stop a negative legacy from infiltrating our children's lives, but we must first identify it.

Positive legacies

Positive legacies are those wonderful things you carry forward that your parents handed on to you. If your parents valued time with you as a child and, for example, made dinner times an important daily event in the family, you might continue that tradition in your own family. Dinner time might now be a technology-free zone, where all members of the family get the opportunity to express what happened to them during the day. Your children will grow and as they move off into their adult lives and form their own families, they will continue that wonderful tradition.

Think for a moment about the positive values, beliefs and traditions you were handed down from the family you grew up in. Are you handing them on to your children? If not, what is causing them to end with you? Maybe your partner's legacy is different from yours, and that is disrupting your efforts to carry on the wonderful tradition you experienced? Whatever the cause, it is important to reflect on the positive legacy you experienced and to become more intentional about bringing it into your life.

Ask yourself the following questions.

- What would I like my children to say about their time living with me?
- What values, beliefs and traditions would I like them to have when they leave?
- What will get in the way of those being positive?

One of the greatest legacies from my own family was that my parents would take us out of school if it was a sunny day. Those were wonderful moments, making sandwiches and packing the car for a day down in Inchydoney, West Cork. That really taught me that you don't have to rigidly follow the rules. And I have passed that on to my children. Those are golden moments, when we head off for a day of fun while the world is busy carrying on with its inflexible routine.

Identifying the positive legacies you experienced, and bringing them into your own family, will create a tradition that you will be proud of in the future. They don't have to be huge gestures, sometimes the small things matter most to children. I had a client tell me that she and her mother always went to the Shelbourne the day before Christmas Eve for afternoon tea. She said they did this for as long as she could remember. When her mother died, she continued that tradition and now makes it an annual event with her own children.

These little things that we enshrine in tradition are sustaining gifts that we hand on to our children. I see the influence these positive legacies have on children. They are more confident, more grounded and have greater self-belief. Their happiness does not rely on external factors, and their peers look up to them. People notice when you believe in yourself and don't simply follow the crowd. And that comes from having parents who handed down positive legacies that supported and allowed you to develop and become autonomous.

Adolescence can be a very difficult time, because children are attempting to assert their autonomy and agency within the confines and rules of family and society. That can be a perplexing experience for a child. How do you attain agency while simultaneously obeying the rules of family and society? That intricate dance can cause huge problems in families. But if managed well, it can help develop a child's sense of self and sense of others. Autonomy is such an important gift to give your child, because the child who believes they are self-governing, with the ability to regulate themselves, is a child who is confident and self-oriented. I meet so many families where the child has failed to mature and develop a strong sense of self. When a child feels they lack agency, it provokes anxiety. Agency is the belief that you have control over your actions. If the development of agency and autonomy are disrupted, it can impact the child long into their adult life.

Negative legacies

There might be some family values, beliefs or traditions that need to be modified or left in the past. For example, you might have been raised by parents who had very narrow ideas about sexuality or race. They might have been quick to judge others, and perhaps you often felt like you were a disappointment to them. They might have been severe in their punishments and refused to allow you to express yourself. There are many different negative legacies you can inherit, but that doesn't mean you have to live with them.

There can be a good outcome from a scenario such as this: now that you are a parent yourself, you can decide that you don't want to subject your children to the same legacy of judgement, discipline and myopic views. Therefore, you consciously ensure that your children don't ever feel like a disappointment. You allow them to express their feelings, and you validate their opinions. This is how a negative legacy can motivate us to be better parents.

This isn't always the case, however. Sometimes, we unconsciously carry negative behaviours that were modelled for us into our adult lives. I often meet parents who are puzzled as to why they act a certain way when their child annoys them. It's like a blind spot – they simply can't see the legacy of the past in themselves. But it's always there. That is why your genogram is a key tool for awareness – once you have awareness, you can make informed choices.

The paradox of negative legacy

Through clinical work, I've come to realize that there is a third possibility here. You can have a good outcome to a negative legacy (motivation) or a bad outcome (blindly repeating it), or you can be so hyperaware of that legacy, you end up bringing the same outcome into your own family. I call this the paradox of negative legacy.

A good example is the person who felt unloved as a child, so as a parent says 'I love you' constantly. The child hears it so often, they can't hear it. It becomes valueless. They feel unloved. Or let's say you were raised in a strict family and you felt it crushed your spirit, so you decide to do the opposite and give in to all your child's needs and wants. This develops in your child an unrealistic expectation that the world will always suit them, and they become too difficult to parent. You cannot understand what has happened, because you did everything to validate their experience.

I see this regularly in my clinic. A familiar narrative is the family who are struggling to understand why the child they value and encourage isn't thriving. They can't understand what is happening, because they are giving their child all the attention they never got and pushing them to succeed in life. The child describes a family unit where they feel isolated and alone because their parent is so focused on them, they can't move. As we delve deeper into the dynamic, the parent explains that they see themself in their child and feel they know what the child needs in order to make something out of their life. Obviously, what they are doing is attempting to parent their own early childhood self. The parent feels the child is unappreciative, because they never got what they are giving their child, but the child feels claustrophobic and a disappointment to the parent, and that makes them deeply unhappy. The same feelings are being experienced through the generations.

This can be incredibly disturbing for a parent: to work so hard to change their childhood and give their child the attention they missed out on, only to realize they have brought the same outcome into their child's life. That is the paradox of a negative family legacy, and it is something to consider if there is tension in your family system.

One of the most disempowering experiences that can happen to us as children is to have all obstacles removed while we navigate our childhood. I have seen it time and time again: college students and adults sitting in my clinic, confused because they feel powerless and don't know how to manage the normal challenges of life. They all tell the same story: parents who were loving and helped them to a degree that made their independence redundant. Of course, it comes from a very well-intentioned parent, but it nonetheless robs the child of their sense of self.

Generally, when I speak with the parents, they describe their own problematic childhood and the desire to ameliorate their experience of ineffectual parenting. It is something I have seen too many times in my clinic for it not to be a truth: often, in our endeavour to rectify some perceived slight or wrongdoing, we over-correct and bring the very thing we are trying to prevent into our lives. Think about how we teach our children to cross the road. We stand at the traffic lights, we show them the cars and explain they are dangerous, we teach them to press the button and be patient, then to cross with the green man. We wouldn't dream of telling our children, 'Don't worry about the cars, I'll always be here to hold your hand, so you don't need to ever think about crossing on your own.' We wouldn't say that because we know they will have to cross the road on their own at some point, so we give them the skill set needed to accomplish that without us.

The cars are a metaphor for adversity and, like the cars, the difficult times will come and go. If children don't learn that, the potential for calamity in adult life is increased, massively. But think of the person who would tell their children that they will always be there to help them. Why would someone say that? To be the hero in their child's life? Whose needs are they meeting? And what are they doing to their child?

Think about your own family of origin: did you have a parent who took those golden learning moments from you? Have a look at your genogram, pull out a moment in your formative life that you know was significant, and look at how your parent reacted in that moment. This is not about blaming your parents but about understanding that sometimes, over the course of our development, our agency might have been taken from us, which will impact our ability to succeed in adulthood. But once we know that, we can start to build it back and become aware of the traps that are waiting for us. Adversity is a normal experience. We will all face it over the course of our lives, but if we have been given the incorrect message that we will never encounter it, because we are too special to face something difficult, then we are going to struggle in adulthood.

—

CASE STUDY
'I know what's best for you'

Kate and her family came to me because her daughter was becoming difficult at home. Both parents attended the session. During the conversation I asked who their daughter was more like. They both agreed she was like her mother. I explained that when we see something in our child that reminds us of ourselves, we can often be motivated to 'fix' whatever we felt we needed help with when we were children.

That sentence really struck Kate and she started to describe how no one had pushed her to achieve her academic dreams. Quite the opposite. She was told she wasn't bright and to forget about college. As a result of this, she pushed back against her parents and left her family home at an early age. That experience was now motivating her to push her daughter to achieve academically. Kate was going to make sure her daughter didn't feel like she did as a child. She was trapped in the paradox of parenting: focusing so hard on her negative experience that she was, unwittingly, re-creating it for her child. Her daughter was now pushing back against her parents, and against Kate in particular. This was causing Kate incredible pain, because all she was trying to do was protect her daughter from a past childhood experience she didn't want her to have.

In that conversation Kate had a breakthrough in understanding her motivations and parenting style. She realized that she could support her daughter and encourage her, without the need to desperately push her. Her experience in childhood wasn't her daughter's – and didn't have to be. After this insight, both parents reported a massive improvement in their relationship with their daughter.

—

What you can do

When children feel pushed, they will often resist. It can be their only power. Ask yourself the following questions.

- Which parent is my child more like?
- Does my partner identify closely with the child?
- Does this motivate the child in a way that is causing tension in the house?

Changing family legacies

If some of what you have just read makes sense to you, and you have found over the years that you and your partner are frequently at odds over how to parent your children – or maybe you wonder why you are incredibly frustrated with your children – it could be a sign that it is time to examine some of your underlying beliefs or values. Once you become aware of the positive and negative family legacies in your life and in your partner's life, you can analyse them and choose which ones you want to keep, discard or modify.

This isn't easy, though, I recognize that. I had a parent tell me recently: 'I couldn't believe the words that came out of my mouth, but when she walked away from me, I shouted at her, "Not in my house you don't, young lady." Those were my mother's words any time we fought. I can't believe I said them.'

The problem is this: the behaviours and values that were handed to you might not be very easy to see, and when you do see them, you can often feel powerless to alter them. But you are not powerless. When you are learning new behaviours, you can often fall back on old, entrenched habits. That can make you feel unable to change. But change is not a straight line. Carl Jung described the 'circumambulation of the self'. In other words, how change is more of a circling motion; we move forward and we move backwards, again and again, but each time we move a little further forward. It is very important to understand this, when you are attempting to improve and bring new behaviours into your life, and to leave some old habits and behaviours behind.

By consciously overwriting some of the negative messages you unconsciously absorbed as a child, replacing them with healthier, more positive ones, you will become more congruent and will start bringing your actions in line with how you want to live. Your life will feel more authentic. Your levels of happiness will increase, too, because you are passing on a positive legacy to your children – one that they will warmly recall in years to come.

For years, we can get stuck living out the legacy of our family unconsciously. When two people come together, their belief systems and values can be in direct conflict – like the same poles of two magnets, they can repel each other. It can be very confusing for a couple as they struggle to parent their children in a meaningful way. One parent is trying to be the child's friend, while the other parent attempts to discipline the children. The children are living with mixed messages, and chaos soon envelops the family unit. I have met so many decent and good people in my clinic who are living in this kind of disharmony. The important first step is to figure out the historical legacy of your family of origin, so that you can become more aligned as a couple and as parents.

What you can do

If one or both of your parents was a source of sorrow and pain, draw their genogram. Take time to think about what life was like for them.

- What was their position in the family? What were their attachments like to their parents?
- What did they learn about love and being a parent from watching their parents live together?
- What type of parent did they want to be? What got in the way of that?

When you start to answer these questions, you begin to see the human being behind your difficult memories.

We often think in such black-and-white terms about someone who has hurt us; it's easier to do that, but it allows the pain to linger. When we see someone who has let us down or caused us pain as a human being who made mistakes, it allows us to forgive them. That is such an important starting point for your healing process. Forgiveness often has religious connotations, in the sense of pardoning someone, but it's not about letting them off the hook, it's about letting go so that the pain leaves you. We hold on to so much, and all those memories – no matter how much we think we have buried them – are still present in our lives. Allowing yourself to let go of them through forgiveness will be one of the most significant processes in your life.

YOUR GENOGRAM

On your genogram, you have already noted your parents' major attachment style with their parents, and their attachment style with you. Now let's move on to the next generation.

1. Write in your attachment style with your own child(ren) – is it the same, is the pattern repeating? Does that make you happy or unhappy? Would you like to change the way you relate to your own child(ren)?
2. Write down any memories that really stick in your head, the ones that crop up whenever you think of your childhood. What do they tell you about your early experiences and lessons? Is there anything you need to rewrite or let go of from your childhood?

PART EIGHT

The Science of Thriving

THERE WAS ONE MEMORY THAT TROUBLED ME FOR MANY YEARS. My father had just come back into the family home after being thrown out by my mother for his affair. He was on his best behaviour for about two weeks, but he couldn't sustain it.

One night, I came home in the early hours from a nightclub, quietly let myself in, climbed the stairs and went into my room. Suddenly, the door flew open, rattling on its hinges, having been kicked so hard. He was screaming at me about coming in so late. This, from the guy who often never came home at all. I picked up my baseball bat and swung it at him, just missing him. I don't think I tried to hit him, but I certainly wanted to set down a marker – you no longer get to kick my door open and threaten me with violence.

It was about 4.00 a.m. I left the house. I walked for hours and ended up down by my old secondary school in Rochestown. I was trying to process what I could do. My brothers had left home, and I was stuck there. I loved my mother and grandmother and didn't want to leave them, but I couldn't stay in that environment much longer. I knew it was destroying me. What could I do?

That moment played in my mind a lot in the years that followed. It was an image of powerlessness and hopelessness. I could easily access those feelings any time I thought about it. But over the years, I began to rewrite the memory and its associated feelings. Perhaps I wasn't a weak, vulnerable child in that moment. Perhaps, walking to my old school about five kilometres away, that was the moment I started to plan my way out of that house. It could be seen as the start of my journey into adulthood, which was a much happier place for me. There can often be a gap in time between decision and action. I didn't make a break for it after that, not for some time. In fact, my depression worsened in the coming years as my father left the house again. The time frame of all this is muddled in my mind. It was a difficult time. I withdrew from friends. In those times, it felt like happiness was a distant possibility – one too far away to ever enter my life.

The seeds that had been sown that night, when I walked for hours, finally made their way to the surface on one horrible night. I asked my father to help me with a debate I was working on. It ended up in name-calling. He liked to throw names at me, derogatory comments about my diagnosis for depression. I knew I wasn't depressed. I knew my family life was depressing. Big difference. He threw a glass of water in my face and told me to take a pill when I became annoyed about it. I'd had enough. I kicked the electric fire in his direction, in a moment of complete frustration and anger. I didn't want to physically fight my father – I don't think anyone really does – but as I walked away he punched me on the side of my face. I'd had enough of his drinking, his lies, his aggression, and now he had just hit me. I turned around, I told my mother to step away, and I hit him.

My grandmother came running out of her room at the sound of the commotion. The scene that greeted her is etched in my memory: my father was on the ground and I was standing over him, like Ali standing over Liston, ordering him to get up. He didn't.

And then I left the house.

I have a large scar on my right hand, reminding me every day of that scene. I hit my father and broke my hand. I needed an operation to fix the tendons that had become dislodged in that fight. I hated myself for that scene. I felt terrible that I had hurt my father. I'll never forget sitting in A&E that night. Lost. Not knowing what to do.

Those are difficult memories – but over time, I have been able to reinterpret them in positive terms. Now, they speak to me of resilience, of a strong sense of self, of determination, of a strong will to survive and to thrive. I had to come to the understanding that happiness wasn't out there on the horizon, forever beyond my reach, it was inside me. I just had to learn where to look.

16. *What is happiness?*

This might sound like an obvious question, but what does happiness look like for you? I have found that the majority of people I talk to in my clinic struggle to put a definition on 'happiness' and really do not have a clear idea of what it is they are striving for. It's worth thinking about this carefully, because searching for something when you don't know what it is and can't recognize it when you see it, causes considerable frustration and despair. It's ultimately exhausting and deflating in equal measure. You have to pin down what it is that makes you happy, and then you can work to bring it into your life.

In terms of the science of happiness, all of the research points to the same thing: happiness is found in your relationship with yourself and with others. It isn't found in wealth and material gain. Every study finds the same conclusion: once you have enough to meet your needs, like food and shelter, happiness doesn't really shift. There is very little difference, if at all, in happiness levels between someone earning €70,000 a year and someone earning €5 million a year. In fact, attaining wealth can often prove a very unhappy reality. The thing you thought would be the source of all happiness can prove to be a false promise.

A study from Northwestern University in Illinois exploring happiness levels between people on ordinary incomes and those who won big prizes in the lottery found that, after the initial spike of increased happiness, within a year there was no difference between the two groups. That kind of happiness is remarkably short-lived. Think about something you were really excited about buying: how long did that feeling last? External sources of happiness do not lead to a sustained increase in happiness levels.

The philosopher Jeremy Bentham's famous definition of happiness as 'the sum of pleasures and pains' captures the tricky balancing act we have to negotiate to attain happiness. According to Bentham, we aggregate the pains and the pleasures of life to arrive at our evaluation of personal happiness. I think it's a little bit more complicated than that.

My own definition is quite simple: I consider the gap between our internalized standard (that which we perceive will make us happy) and reality (that which we have). The smaller the gap between our internalized standard and reality, the greater our chance of happiness. By gaining better insights into what makes us happy, not just our perceived notions of happiness, we can increase our levels of happiness.

It's all about how you choose to define happiness for yourself – no comparisons to others, no unrealistic standards. If you develop a realistic and more sophisticated internalized standard of happiness – for example, improving social relationships, connecting to family, being more authentic, thinking about others, improving levels of openness – those are goals that you have power over.

Whenever I'm giving talks on this issue, I break happiness into four pillars:

1. your relationship with your body
2. your relationship with your friends and family
3. your relationship with work
4. your internal relationship with yourself.

When you start to look at these pillars, you can become more specific about how to increase your levels of happiness. Generally, in my experience, not every aspect of life is going badly. Clients often selectively focus on one area, and that becomes the narrative for their entire life experience. To avoid this, score each of these pillars out of ten, to identify which needs your attention. (You'll find more detail on tracking your happiness levels in Chapter 18: 'Break down your obstacles to happiness'.)

Personality and happiness

Research shows that the personality traits of extraversion and openness lead to happier lives. Now, that doesn't mean if you are introverted you can't be happy – of course you can be – but you can cultivate those particular traits to increase your internal happiness. You can work on increasing your level of openness.

An important question to ask is, why are we capable of happiness? The answer lies in the fact that when we are happy, we are better able to meet the demands of life, to think creatively, and be more flexible in our thinking. These are very important attributes for our survival as a species. When you are open to life and all it has to offer, more positive things come into your life. When more positive things come into your life, you will be happier. It's like the sieve I described in Chapter 11 ('Addiction and the family'): when you are closed off from the potential of positive things happening, only negative experiences can get through. I hear so many clients declare, 'Why does nothing good ever happen to me?' A mindset that has come to this conclusion cannot experience something good happening. It is impossible. This means the individual lives out this awful, self-fulfilling prophecy.

The brain and happiness

When we are unhappy, our thinking becomes rooted in a negative thought or memory. We become rigid, the opposite of open, and our world shrinks. Remember what I said earlier about depression and memory: scientific research shows that a depressed person has heightened negative memory recall. The mental sieve is only letting the bad through.

We generally have two types of happiness:

- when good things happen in a specific event, or
- when we positively evaluate our life and accomplishments overall.

The second type of happiness is more sustaining. Think about that for a moment: this shows that, far from being simply an increase in positive emotions, there must be a cognitive aspect to happiness. How we recall and interpret our memories is significant for our happiness.

When I was in my early twenties, I viewed my father in a very negative light. I had a myopic viewpoint: *people let you down*. That was not a helpful philosophy. As I grew older, I started to revisit those memories and ideas about who my father was. I started to see him as a complex human being who was flawed, like the rest of us. Those memories no longer held negative power in my life. He ceased to be a dark, brooding presence in the corner of my mind. I started to trust people. This shift dramatically changed my mood and feelings.

Cognitive theories on happiness suggest that happiness is the product of human thinking, and that unhappiness reflects discrepancies between perceptions of life as it is and notions of how life should be. Again, this suggests that being honest and realistic about yourself and your life is an important route to happiness.

Being authentic – the me you see

It is very difficult to love yourself and feel happy when you don't value yourself enough to be authentic and true to who you are. Are you living with an inner self and an outer self? Are they similar, or very different? Is there a gap between how you want to be seen and the self you project? Happiness is massively depleted when there is conflict between the inner and outer selves. If you aren't living your life authentically, you cannot feel happy. That conflict will rub away the good things that happen and leave you feeling constantly ill at ease in the world.

We have to make sure, as much as we can, that who we are internally is aligned with the persona we present to the world. False personae are too much for the psyche to maintain, and they destroy our peace. You can't be happy when the self you present to the world isn't authentic.

What you can do
Do you compare yourself to others? In that comparison, do you find glaring deficits? What do you hold as the standards of a good life? Are they realistic? Do you need to re-evaluate those standards?

If you feel you are not doing as well as others, why do you feel that? Is your interpretation of those other lives an illusion? Is it truly the case that everyone else is blissfully happy while you are struggling?

Try to define what happiness means to you. It is so important that you know what you are striving for. Think about it, then write it down.

Does your definition differ from the definition of happiness you inherited from your family? Happiness is subjective. Each one of us has an internal standard of happiness that we are striving to achieve. Become aware of what has constructed your standard. Ask yourself, can you control any of that standard, or is it rooted in some external force? What would need to change in your life to make happiness more present?

What does unhappiness look like?

You might find this easier to answer. If you are struggling to find your definition of happiness, identifying what it is not can be a good starting point. Think about it, then write down what makes you unhappy.

Let's say your unhappy list looks like this.

I hate it when:

- I'm weak
- I don't stand up for myself
- I shout at the kids or treat my partner with disrespect
- I take on too much, am unable to say no
- I compare myself to others.

Whatever is on your list, avoid that like the plague. No gimmick. Just very simple. And if you stick to it, you will notice your levels of happiness increase, because you are not doing the things that cause you unhappiness. So, at the very least you are not bringing terrible suffering into your life.

That's a good starting point. But it's not easy. You have been doing it for so long, it takes real effort to change. But the rewards are massive. There is a monster industry built around happiness, goading us into taking on board external goals that end up ruling our lives. But the answers to your happiness lie within you, and in your relationships with others. When you control your definition of happiness, that's a much more positive place to be in.

If you want to avoid unhappiness and promote happiness, there are two key guidelines you can follow.

1. Act always in the interest of your future self – this might mean delaying immediate gratification, which is not easy.
2. Look at the four key elements of how you take control of your own happiness:

   • goal
   • effort
   • attainment of goal
   • autonomy.

You set your own goals, you put in the effort required, you attain your goals, and you do all that with a strong sense of autonomy, in other words, in the clear knowledge that you are doing it for yourself. Gaining a sense of agency over your life will free you from feeling like a victim.

We all have 'masters' to some degree – people who are in positions of power in our life. Can we be authentic in front of them? How do we figure out who those masters are? Well, if you have ever wondered who your master is, ask yourself, who are you not able to speak honestly about, for fear of retribution? This will immediately reveal your master. This is an interesting little exercise to do. It should illuminate an important insight, and make you realize that you should not bend your true self to suit the will of someone else, even if they are your boss. When you do this, you give away your agency and you start to lose respect for yourself.

CASE STUDY
The happiness diagnostic tool

One of the most important conversations I have with clients on this topic is getting them to run a diagnostic on their weekly lived experience. I ask them to track their levels of happiness over the course of a week. The following example is taken from a client I was working with. He was forty-two years of age, married, with two children. He came to me because he felt life was passing him by and he didn't feel connected to anything. He recorded his feelings of happiness/unhappiness for a week and awarded each day a happiness score out of ten, with ten being 'Happy' and zero being 'Unhappy'.

Monday: 3/10 Just woke up feeling crap, thought about the week and got sick feeling, didn't feel good all day. Kept to myself. Hate putting kids to bed. Sick of the fights, and then fights with my wife about it.

Tuesday: 2/10 Didn't sleep well, was thinking about my life and relationships. Felt disconnected from everyone.

Wednesday: 4/10 Got a good night's sleep, chatted with some in work, had meal with wife. Felt better. Bedtime wasn't so bad but still I dread bedtime. Wish I didn't feel like that. I feel guilty after I shout at them to be quiet.

Thursday: 6/10 Went out with friends for a drink after work. Met old friends. Came home to nice dinner, had good conversation with wife. Bedtime wasn't so bad, I read them a story, my daughter told me she loves when I read a story, that felt good. Need to do that more.

Friday: 7/10 Woke up feeling good, looking forward to weekend. Thought about taking family out for picnic to zoo. They were excited.

Saturday: 3/10 Had a fight with wife, same old stuff. Was on my own all day. She gave out to me for promising to take kids to zoo. I just didn't have the energy. Didn't go to zoo. Shouted at kids at night, daughter was crying going to sleep, felt like running away.

Sunday: 2/10 Made up with wife, but had sinking feeling I'll never be happy. I can't beat this low feeling. I'm doomed to feeling bad. Had a thought they'd be better off without me.

We went through his tracker together, exploring what caused him to feel low and what made him feel good. It was clear that his connection to others was an important aspect of his happiness, and that his negative predisposition and fatalistic way of looking at things were impacting how he was feeling.

I noticed that his mood was always lower in the morning. I asked him to describe his morning in detail. He told me that he woke at about 5.00 a.m., checked his phone, watched videos on YouTube. When his alarm went off, he felt dread in the pit of his stomach; thoughts of the day ahead were a source of discomfort and unhappiness. He explained this was because the thought that nothing exciting lay ahead made him feel low. He liked his job, but felt trapped in the mundane banality of routine. He acknowledged that his relationship with his wife could be a lot better and that his feelings of disconnection from her and his children were a key source of his unhappiness.

We also looked at why bedtime was particularly difficult, and he said that he was tired and hungry at this time and couldn't understand why the children would push back against him after he had given them so much. He described his own childhood as being a very lonely and negative experience. He wanted to give his children a better life but felt terribly guilty and ashamed that he was shouting and being aggressive with his children.

Based on his happiness tracker and our discussions, I prescribed some actions he could take to tackle his sense of unhappiness.

- Do not use your phone first thing in the morning. Wake up to radio alarm clock – tune in white noise and allow that gentle sound to pull you out of sleep.
- Write out positive affirmations about the day ahead, such as:

  o *Today something good will happen.*
  o *I am valuable and worthy.*
  o *I love being alive.*
  o *I am a good father.*

- During the course of your day, look for three examples of one of those affirmations occurring and write it down when you come home.
- Put the kids to bed earlier, so that you are not rushing and trying to meet an unrealistic expectation that they will go to sleep immediately. Read them a story each night.
- Do something each day that is spontaneous and different from yesterday. This can be something small, like going somewhere different for lunch.
- Plan a weekend activity with your family and follow through on it. Let your children also plan an activity and do it as a family.
- Meet your friends at least once a week.
- Get exercise – go for a walk / run every second night.
- Get off your devices before 8.00 p.m.
- Improve sleep hygiene. If you had a bad conversation with someone, journal what was said; this will allow you to process that argument and prevent rumination at night.

He went away for a week with a promise to try to embed these tips into his daily life. His following week's tracker, covering six days, looked like this:

Monday: 6/10 Find waking up by radio much better, and not looking at videos makes me feel a lot more refreshed. Even went for a walk before work.

Tuesday: 3/10 Went on phone first thing. Shouldn't have it in room. Feel guilty. Had same old fight with kids about bedtime. Didn't read story.

Wednesday: 7/10 Went for a walk during lunch today and bought tickets for play. Told wife about weekend and she was thrilled I showed initiative. Put kids to bed earlier and read them story.

Thursday: 8/10 Went to gym during lunch. Met few friends after work. Felt really good coming home. Thought about something my daughter said to me last night, 'I love when you read stories.' That was lovely. Looking forward to Saturday. Do more of that.

Friday: 8/10 Did something spontaneous at lunch, went to park and sat down and read a bit of a book I bought. Put kids to bed earlier and read story. My son told me a joke he heard in school. Feel more connected to them.

Saturday: 9/10 Went for a run. Had a great night at play, nice meal. Had great conversation with wife. She said she has noticed a difference in me. That was great to hear. I just feel more connected to my family.

He moved from a weekly score of 27/70 (38 per cent) to 41/60 (68 per cent). A 30 per cent increase in one week is substantial.

—

You can see how making small changes dramatically alters how we are feeling. Our personality traits directly impact the standards we devise with regard to our happiness; those standards, in turn, directly impact our comparative cognition (the way we view our life and compare ourselves with others). This is what gives us a sense of either power or powerlessness to bring about change in our lives. When we analyse those components together, we come to a sense of our overall happiness.

What you can do

Track your happiness for a week, following the scale given above. Make a note each day. At the end of the week, add up your score and analyse the data. Which days were better? What was happening on those days? What needs to change to improve your score?

Make the necessary adjustments for the following week, and track your happiness again. Analyse the data and see if the percentage of happiness has improved.

It is vitally important that you analyse what is happening on the days you don't feel so good, and what is happening on the days when you are feeling better. Making a note of what is happening in your life when you are feeling good, and intentionally doing more of that, could be a simple yet life-altering exercise. Do less of what makes you feel bad, and do more of those things that make you feel good. We all know this, but it is often the simplest things we find hardest to implement.

YOUR GENOGRAM

1. Go back to your genogram and think about your internalized standard for happiness. Where do you think that came from?
2. Look at your parents' genogram and write next to both your parents what their internalized standard for happiness was. Did it shape yours?

Often, clients tell me about how materialistic their parents were and how they are not like them, yet they also speak of how they envy a neighbour or friend who is doing so well financially. They have learned that happiness is found in materialism, and while they say it is a false premise, they are still caught living it and not enjoying life. If this is happening to you, you need to be honest and identify it clearly.

---

17. The key components of well-being

Now that you have created your own personal definition of happiness, tracked your levels of happiness over the course of a week, and made important adjustments by doing more of what makes you feel good, it is time to get a more detailed and nuanced understanding of what we need to think about when we attempt to improve our well-being.

In psychology, we identify five key components of well-being. You need to be aware of these and how they impact your life, from childhood onwards. Once you are aware of them, you will need to consciously promote them in your daily life in order to increase your levels of happiness. The higher your level of each of these, the happier you will be. They are:

- autonomy and agency
- openness
- connection
- writing your own narrative
- purpose/meaning.

Autonomy and agency

Autonomy means the ability to self-govern, while agency means the control you feel over your actions. These components drive you in childhood and adolescence to strive to gain a sense of yourself as a separate and independent individual.

When the early attachment is secure, the child develops its sense of autonomy in a healthy way, through exploration and feedback. Their explorations always start from a safe harbour, and they know they can return there at any time. That sense of safety is what allows them to enter unsafe territory; they can explore far and wide, knowing their home berth is waiting for them. Autonomy gives you a sense of competency. You understand that life won't always go your way, but you have skills that you can utilize when things get rough, and that's an empowering realization.

When the early attachment is insecure, it changes how the baby acts and how it comes to perceive the world. When the environment you grow up in is unsafe or ruled by a despot, and you feel you cannot freely express yourself, this has a deleterious impact on levels of autonomy. The child comes to understand they have to shape-shift in order to survive their environment. Failure to develop agency can lead to a child doubting their own abilities and developing feelings of shame. When a child becomes autonomous, they are able to discover and acquire new skills. They are free to explore the world and make mistakes.

Autonomy has two vital aspects:

- an emotional component, where you rely more on yourself than your parents, and
- a behavioural component, where you make decisions independently by using your judgement.

The ability to make decisions is a key part of autonomy. Are you riddled by indecision? Do you over-analyse every little aspect of a decision, eventually not acting for fear you might make the wrong decision? This could be down to a low level of autonomy.

The style of child-rearing and the family dynamic affect the development of a child's sense of autonomy. Autonomy in adolescence is closely related to the quest for identity. In adolescence, parents and peers act as agents of influence. Peer influence in early adolescence may help the adolescent to gradually become more autonomous by being less susceptible to parental influence as they get older. The most important developmental task in adolescence is to develop a healthy sense of autonomy. In adulthood, failure to feel autonomous can lead to a significant decrease in happiness.

Someone who has high levels of autonomy is self-determined and independent. They can resist social pressures to think and act a certain way, they regulate behaviours from within, and they evaluate themself and their achievements by personal standards. This means they can still be autonomous and work in a job they really don't care for.

Someone who has low levels of autonomy is too concerned with the expectations of others, relies on the judgements of other people to make important decisions, and conforms to social pressures to think and act in certain ways. They feel like they need to constantly shift their opinions to suit the crowd.

Children often present as duplicitous when they have low levels of autonomy. I have often heard teachers describe children as 'sneaky'. All behaviour is communication, and that type of child generally has had to shape-shift to manage their environment. Adults with low autonomy can struggle to find their authentic voice, they go along with things they don't agree with, and they often become resentful of themselves. Lack of autonomy is a thief of joy.

How to strengthen autonomy

- *Develop your competencies.* The more skills you have, the more autonomy you will gain. The less you are dependent on one source of income or one person, the more you gain freedom. That doesn't mean that to be happy you need more than one income source but, in my experience, not allowing yourself to be governed by one skill or person makes you powerful and gives you options. In my clinic, people often describe feeling trapped; they are stuck in their job because they feel they have no options or potential to grow.
- *Develop the ability to say no.* This is crucial for autonomy. Why is it some people can say no to things they don't want to do, while others feel they have to say yes to everything in order to be valued? The difference is a strong sense of autonomy.
- *Get comfortable with other people's discomfort.* When you become more autonomous, people close to you might often push back because you are changing the

homeostasis of an old family dynamic. Don't allow this to sway you.

- *Express yourself honestly.* This will develop your sense of self. You will start to like yourself. That is very empowering.

Openness

We met openness in the 'Big Five' personality traits (see Chapter 6: 'Personalities at play within the family') and we learned that high levels of openness improve your levels of happiness. Openness is all about embracing new things, fresh ideas and novel experiences. The more you are open to new things, the more new and exciting things happen in your life. Openness generates more positive experiences.

During our formative years, if we experience something very negative or traumatic, we can come to view the world through a very cynical lens. That hurt child develops a philosophy, reiterated constantly by a destructive internal voice, to protect themself from future calamity: 'Don't expect anything good to ever happen to you, that way you won't be let down.' I have heard this self-fulfilling prophecy so many times in my clinic.

People with low levels of openness tend to be very rigid, cautious and often unable to deal with change. I had a teenage girl recently explain that she speaks negatively to herself as a protection against hurtful comments: 'If I was feeling great and someone said something terrible to me, that would hurt too much.' That is the voice of a girl who has closed herself off in order to protect herself. But her unhelpful intervention ensures she is hurting all the time. The very thing she fears the most is the thing she brings into her life.

People who are not open tend to stay in jobs they do not like. They are fearful of what will happen if they change; they feel they don't have the competency to manage change and what that might bring into their life. They often miss opportunities because they cannot see them right in front of their eyes. In my experience, they often have a fear of thriving. Their perspective has become narrowed, and all they see is their limitations, not the possibilities that await them.

We need to be flexible, because change is all around us. Openness is a gift – I have learned that in my own life. I came from a place where I built walls in an attempt to be 'untouchable', but it was an illusion. I had to break down those walls and let the light in. This is what openness is all about – opening yourself up to the possibility of something new coming into your life and, crucially, being able to see it when it does, because your mindset can let that light in.

How to strengthen openness

- *Push yourself to learn something new.* What interest have you never found the time to explore? Let's say you always had an interest in playing the guitar or piano. Now is the time to give that a go. Open people are open to learning new things, they make the time, and it enriches their lives considerably.
- *Be open to new things.* People who have low levels of openness tend to avoid new experiences, which shrinks their life down to repeated, familiar patterns. For example, they go on the same holiday every year. Explore somewhere new, or embrace a new experience on holiday. Travel opens the mind and makes you more open to meeting new people and having new experiences.
- *Do something spontaneous during your week.* Life can become a series of mundane familiar routines, where we can predict with accuracy what will happen on any given day. Routine is important, but too much of it can erode creativity and numb the soul. Be daring, disturb your universe and do something spontaneous, no matter how small.

Connection

Whenever I think of my childhood holidays, I have this image of old Frenchmen playing boules, sitting out in short-sleeved shirts, sipping small glasses of beer. There is something warm about that memory. They are together, laughing, chatting, lost in the game. Irish culture is different, and I think Irish men and women often struggle to stay connected to their friends as life becomes more complicated in middle age. Yet all the research points to the simple fact that the more we are connected to those we love, the more we experience happiness.

I can verify this from the other side: I meet so many clients who have lost that sense of connection and are deeply unhappy as a result. Their lives feel isolated and separate. So many married women in my clinic describe a sense of isolation and loneliness. Intimacy has depleted significantly, they are caught in endless responsibilities, and they pass their partner like ships on a dark ocean, rarely taking time to connect with each other. Children grow up and move on. What will survive them must be your love for each other. Don't allow that to get lost in the dance of parenting. It is easy to forget why you brought these children into the world in the first place: to share your relationship with them.

—

CASE STUDY
Living in silence

I saw a young teenage boy who was sent to me because he was suffering with dysthymia, persistent low depression. He was very flat in our first conversation. It wasn't until we spoke about living in his parents' relationship that he broke down, describing the atmosphere in the house.

When I spoke to his parents, they both agreed that his description of tension and silence was accurate. They explained how the relationship had deteriorated in recent years. We had a family session, and the youngest daughter, who was nine years old, said she hated living with the silences. She was a remarkable young girl, able to articulate so vividly the separation each member of family was experiencing. There were no dinner-time conversations, meals were eaten separately, no connection in the morning, the evenings were spent in bedrooms, away from each other.

The teenage boy said it wasn't until he went and stayed at a friend's house that he realized why he was so sad. He watched in shock as his friend's father played with them, and then they all sat down together for dinner and chatted about their day.

What that teenage boy witnessed in his friend's house was connection. His own family were disconnected from one other, and it was causing him great sadness.

—

I remember so vividly the feeling of disbelief when I had dinner with my first real girlfriend's family, when I was about sixteen. I remember asking her, 'Does your dad ever get really angry and throw stuff around?' I immediately regretted asking, because I could see by her reaction that she didn't know what I was talking about. That often happens to us: we accept the reality we are born into, until we see the reality of others and our perception changes irrevocably.

Connection is essential for our well-being and also for a healthy family system. Disconnection puts everything out of kilter, and we suffer as a result.

How to strengthen connection

- *Be more intentional about your friendships.* Ensure you spend time regularly with your family and friends.
- *Allow your child(ren) to pick a family activity.* They derive great joy from seeing the family enjoying their suggested outing. It enhances their sense of self, their autonomy, and forges those connections between family members.
- *Reach out.* If you have lost a friend over the years, due to the busyness of life, reconnect with them. Reach out and arrange to meet them. This might be one of the most important things you do, as you will potentially bring an important friend back into your life.
- *Fix your disconnections.* If you have a rupture in your relationship with a sibling, try to fix it. Now that you have a detailed genogram of your lives and perspectives, maybe you can view their position a little differently? Try not to

think about who is to blame, but reach out, reconnect and move on.

Writing your own narrative

The story you tell yourself about who you are is the most important story you will ever hear. Unfortunately, we are hard-wired to look for negatives, that is a primitive survival mechanism. Constantly looking for threat kept us alive in our early adventure as human beings, so we are primed to see negativity all around us. As a result, talking positively to ourselves can be a real challenge. I hear so many beautiful and talented young teenagers, both boys and girls, talk about themselves in such destructive language. The age of social media has increased cognitive comparison and made it harder to have a positive internal voice. I meet many people who are incredibly compassionate and caring towards others, but they don't show themselves the same levels of care and compassion. People are often so intolerant of themselves.

If you tell yourself a negative story about who you are and what you are capable of, you need to recognize this and rewrite that story. Figure out why that narrative developed in the first place. We often talk negatively to ourselves because we believe it might cause a positive outcome. But that negative worry voice doesn't change any future outcome, it just ruins your present. That's a significant trade-off. We can all rewrite the story of who we are, so that we think in a more positive light.

How to improve your personal narrative

- *Assess your internal voice.* Is it a friend? Does it support you? Or does it subjugate and diminish you? What was the last thing it said to you? How you would like that voice to sound? What could it say to you that would lift you up and propel you forward in a positive way?
- *Write out three things that you would like to say about yourself.* For example:

o I am worthy.
o I am loved.
o I am beautiful.

Now look for instances in your life that act as proof of these things. Write them down.

Purpose/meaning

Finding meaning and purpose in this multifaceted, fast-paced world can be a real challenge. We have bills to pay, responsibilities to meet, we have to compromise on many of the things we would like to do. Often, we are chasing the wrong things, and when we finally achieve them, the emptiness experienced shocks us profoundly. I have heard so many clients utter the same thing after they have lost so much in the pursuit of other things: 'It was right in front of me all the time.' They had ignored their sources of true happiness and embarked on a fool's errand.

In my life, being with my family and watching my children grow up gives me incredible joy. At times, though, I have to really work at appreciating it, because it is so easy to take it all for granted. I think that's the same for all of us. We have to strive to remain conscious of what gives us the greatest sense of meaning, of what the truest purpose is in our lives.

Neuroscience tells us that thoughts about the self are statistically indistinguishable from negative feelings and emotions. What this means is that the more we think about ourselves, the more unhappy we are going to be. Nothing exemplifies the current era of human existence more than the 'selfie'. It is looking inwards, it is pointed at the self. We need to start looking outwards if we are to find true meaning in our lives. Doing things for others and helping people is such an important aspect of meaning and happiness.

How to promote meaningfulness

- *Take time to appreciate things.* What could you appreciate more about your life?
- *Recognize what brings you joy.* What aspect of your life gives it meaning? Can you amp up that aspect?
- *Start looking outwards.* What could you do that would help others?
- *Identify the things you are chasing.* Sometimes we lose sight of what is really important, but focusing on what you have in life and developing gratitude for that can give a deep sense of meaning.

YOUR GENOGRAM

Your genogram is a vital tool for looking at some of the key components of your well-being.

1. Go back to your attachment style for a moment: how do you think it impacted your sense of autonomy and agency?
2. Is there anyone on your genogram you would like to have a better connection with? What is stopping you from deepening that relationship? Look at what you have filled in about them on your genogram: would their life be better with you in it?
3. Ask yourself, if your relationship with someone you love was closer and/or that conflict was healed, would it positively impact their life and your life?

18.   *Break down your obstacles to happiness*

By this stage, you have done a lot of work on your genogram and thinking about your past life, your personality, your strengths and weaknesses, working towards identifying what you want to improve and what you want to change. We all know that change is never easy – even when it's badly needed and wanted. It takes effort and discipline. And here's the crux of the matter: you are your own greatest agent of change, but you can also be your own greatest obstacle to change.

I have listened to so many clients explain to me how they are terrified to flourish. They have been talking negatively to themselves their entire life and they can't imagine talking positively to themselves. It would change that inner voice, which is so familiar they can't imagine life without it. It would mean taking control over who they become, which in turn would mean being responsible for who they are.

Does this sound familiar to you? Is there something you've always had an interest in but put it off because you are busy? Was that the true reason? Did you perhaps put it off because you are frightened of trying – of failing, of succeeding? You have been telling yourself the story of who you are and what you are capable of for so long, would it feel strange and uncomfortable to re-author that story and become more positive and powerful? What would happen if you actually started to thrive? Would that be scary?

Connecting with your true self and casting off some of the old ideas that have hindered you could be that first true moment of happiness in your life. But it is so often the case that we are fearful of that change and all it would entail. Fear is an extremely powerful obstacle, and it usually disguises itself – we heap other reasons on top of it and don't realize what lies beneath them. So, the first step is to understand how fear works in your life, then you can dismantle it.

How we live in fear

There are three key responses to fear:

- avoidance
- control
- seeking reassurance.

How we were raised can have a direct impact on our fear response. If you had an avoidant attachment style in early development, it can programme you to avoid feelings and difficult situations. This early experience taught you that negative things should be avoided. This can often play out in a very destructive way as an adult.

We avoid the fear

The more powerless we feel, the more we cling to avoidance as a strategy. Feeling powerless can manifest itself in our daily lived experience. If we believe we have no power to change a particular situation, we might choose to simply avoid it. We can do this by pushing it away and refusing to think about it, or we can literally avoid it – for example, by refusing to meet a particular person. This avoidance doesn't change the situation, it just offers some protection from those difficult feelings of powerlessness and lack of agency. It is interesting to note that patterns of avoidance are the source of phobic behaviour.

Avoid avoiding at all costs. Be mindful of the solutions you choose to tackle the problems in your life. Look at your solution choices up until this point. It's easy to get stuck using the same old solutions, and then nothing changes. That can cause a sense of hopelessness. You can change how you tackle problems, but first you have to analyse your solutions. If they are not working, stop using them. Remember that problem-solving is modelled for us by our parents, and they might be using failed solutions that were modelled by their parents.

Avoidance can be such a subtle and invisible tool used in your daily life to manage problems, difficult people or situations. Think about your life for a moment: do you avoid problems or people? What would it mean to actually stay in the difficulty and not avoid it? Would you learn that you are far more powerful than you thought?

—

CASE STUDY
From avoidance to validation

I had a female client tell me that she avoided going back into her parents' house because they never validated her experience growing up. Her mother was incredibly critical of her as the eldest daughter. Both parents had big careers and had depended on her to mind her siblings. She described a difficult childhood, of responsibility and loneliness.

As we talked and explored her genogram, she started to get a deeper insight into her experience. Her attachment style really helped her to see how she behaved in relation to her childhood experience.

She came into the clinic one morning, looking lighter and visibly happy. She had gone to her parents' house over the weekend and sat with them and explained her experience growing up and how it had affected her adult life. This was the first time she had ever really spoken her feelings on this subject, and it was the first time her parents validated her lived childhood experience.

—

There's an important lesson to learn: when we avoid, we don't validate ourselves, and nor do we give others the opportunity to articulate their side of the experience.

We attempt to control the fear

If you had an anxious attachment style and a high level of neuroticism as a result, you might use control in a pathological way. Control is such an important word for human beings. In Chapter 9 ('Comfortably numb – the power of positive feedback loops') we encountered that very helpful phrase: 'Take control of not having control, and this will give you control.' But you can see that control is used three times in that simple sentence. It's one of the cornerstones of our psychological well-being, but that means we can have huge fears around our perceived sense of control or lack of control.

One of the most common fear responses is attempting to control an uncontrollable situation, which can lead to despair. When we settle into our seat on a plane, we have no control over that flight. The pilot, the engineering, the weather, these are all in control of our life. We must surrender control. But if we cannot do that, or refuse to do that, our brain will create all sorts of answers to that particular problem. If you had a difficult childhood and it was particularly chaotic or dysfunctional, you can often attempt to control every aspect of your adult life. The desire to move away from that childhood experience can motivate you to become incredibly controlling.

You might also attempt to control your emotional responses by not allowing those feelings to emerge. This can really impact your well-being, as all those difficult feelings and experiences remain unprocessed. When you go back into your family home, your parents or siblings might say something to provoke an emotional response from you, but you shut it down in an attempt to control the situation. Every aspect of your life is tightly controlled, but it is like the pressure on a valve: the more you attempt to control it, the more the pressure increases, until eventually it will need release.

Our lives are so complicated, and we often feel out of control. We use different solutions to help manage that complexity. We fear the lack of control and try to control it. But that fear causes our lives to become joyless. When it becomes even more extreme, the attempt to control our fears can lead to obsessive behaviours. Children can develop tics, adults can do things ritualistically, thinking in patterns, praying or ruminating on ideas or situations. All of these strategies for attempting to regain control bring suffering into a person's life. They are positive feedback loops.

—

CASE STUDY
Obsessed by fear

I met a young teenage girl in my clinic who had stopped sleeping in her own bed and it was causing the family a considerable amount of distress.

Her father would have to get out of his bed and let her sleep with her mother. She had developed the thought that her bedroom wasn't safe, therefore she could only sleep when she was with her mother. The moment she got into her mother's bed she fell into a deep sleep.

Her parents believed she had a sleep issue, but it ran deeper than that. As with many people who suffer with obsessive behaviours, she had told no one in her life that she had developed obsessive intrusive thoughts, which were driving her behaviour. When I said to her in our first conversation, 'Are you keeping your recurring thoughts and behaviours to yourself?' she looked at me as if I had seen deep into her soul and found something she was ashamed of. She was shocked, but then there was huge relief when she realized she wasn't alone in her thinking.

I explained to her that if she sat with me in my clinic for a week, she would hear so many teenagers talk about counting obsessively or repeating a phrase over and over again. She smiled at me and said, 'That's me.' Immediately, she let me into her world of intrusive thoughts. She couldn't stop checking under the bed, checking all the doors were locked, checking inside her wardrobe, praying obsessively, repeating phrases like a mantra: 'Go away, go away.' This was all in response to the fear that a killer clown would come and murder her. She had also developed the fear that if she didn't count to a particular number, someone she loved would die. She often stayed up all night counting, until she reached the number. Sitting with this wonderful young girl, whose life had collapsed into tyrannical despair, her suffering was difficult to witness.

I gave her a small task to do over the following two weeks. If she was going to check the locks, she had to do the entire routine three times. She couldn't do it twice or four times – she *had* to do it three times. I prescribed this intervention because I wanted to subtly introduce her to the reality that she was choosing this behaviour, that she had control over it, that she wasn't powerless to change it, as she thought. This intervention would take the spontaneity from the behaviour.

The next time I saw her, she told me that after one week of doing this, she had stopped checking the doors. She had slept a little more in her own bed, although she still slept with her mother at times. Slowly we began to dismantle her belief that she needed her mother in order to sleep.

Finally, she had a breakthrough. She said to me, 'I have begun to realize that maybe it's not my room that is the problem, that maybe it's me.' Up until this point she had the belief that the room was tormenting her. Now she was beginning to understand that the actual problem was the way she was managing her stress.

In one of our final sessions, she came into the clinic in very high spirits. She had recently attended a sleepover in a friend's house, something that would have been impossible a couple of weeks earlier. She felt confident and proud of herself. This marked the beginning of the end of intrusive thoughts in her life. In that final session, I told her that those old thoughts might pop up from time to time, but not to fear them.

—

If we are plagued by obsessive behaviours, we need to learn to see them for what they are: a reaction to stress. Once we break the logic that is holding us back, or tormenting us, we can thrive.

We seek reassurance

Reassurance is defined as the removal of someone's doubts or fears. Ironically, in this psychological context, the more a child receives reassurance, the more they become prey to doubts and fears. People can sometimes try to keep fear at bay by asking others they trust to reassure them that what they fear won't happen, that they are safe from it. This becomes a problem when the person develops a reliance on an external force – for example, a mother – to constantly resolve their fears. The more this happens, the more they realize they need that person in order to feel good. This is an incredibly disempowering dynamic. Reassurance can be like kryptonite; it's the thing that is making the child seek reassurance in the first place. The more they get, the more they need, and it becomes an empty pursuit.

When I work in the corporate space, I meet many talented and brilliant people, high functioning, high achieving, but so often struggling with a common dilemma: they need constant reassurance. And the more they get, the more they need, so much so that it almost paralyses them in their ability to function at the level required. They resent themselves for needing reassurance. They see their colleagues making decisions and not seeking reassurance, and it underlines their own inadequacy, which makes them seek reassurance even more. Parents also regularly describe the same problem: the more reassurance they give their child, the more the child needs. What is it about reassurance that can so easily get us caught in a bind?

At the root of needing reassurance can be an anxious attachment style or high levels of neuroticism. We learned early in childhood that things were not secure but were constantly changing. We looked for reassurance to tell us that everything was okay, and when we got it, we felt better for a moment. But then things changed again, and so we needed more reassurance, and on it went. Seeking constant reassurance causes us to believe we don't have the skill set or competency to manage or regulate ourselves. In short, seeking reassurance causes us to dislike ourselves, and that is a huge price to pay for how we deal with a fear.

What you can do

Think about your family of origin. How did your parents deal with emotional disturbances?

What solutions do you use that you know, deep down, are failing you and causing you to feel hopeless? Make a conscious choice to stop using them.

The four aspects of thriving

We all would like to thrive in life, but sometimes we feel like we are standing still – or even going backwards. If you are feeling like this, it's important to figure out what you are doing, or not doing, that is hindering your ability to thrive, then you can work on those aspects to your benefit.

It is difficult to change when you don't know what it is you have to change, or why you think or act a certain way. It's not a case that some people are born with low resilience and others are endowed with an abundance of it. That's simply not the way things work. A multitude of things must occur for us to see ourselves as powerful: we must understand that we are not victims of our childhood, that we had certain attachments that impacted how we experience and perceive the world, that we speak a particular love language, and that we have personality traits that hinder or help us to experience joy.

In other words, becoming powerful means understanding we are the agents of change in our life. We can't expect anyone else to change our lives for us. What we saw modelled as children is significant in how we behave in adult life, but it is not paramount. We are not what happened to us, we are who we choose to become. That is empowering. Yes, our early childhood influences us. Our parents make us optimistic in our thinking and allow us to learn for ourselves, or, if we grew up in dysfunction, this experience shows us how to survive by any means possible. We quickly come to realize that we are not enough, and that we have to change ourselves to adapt quickly to the ever-changing, unpredictable environment we are navigating. We have always lived with a sense of imminent threat, always on high alert. When we are not taught how to manage ourselves in a healthy way, it depletes our reservoir of resilience. But we can learn to change those responses.

We have all seen behaviour modelled as children that we have assimilated and use every day. Remember, the brain is lazy and constantly looking for the familiar. Everything you have done up until this point hasn't killed you, so your brain thinks, 'Well, this works.' It may work, but it may not be working very well for your life. It's important to look at how you approach your life and the life choices you face – are your thoughts and behaviours working to your best advantage?

When clients sit in front of me and describe a sense of hopelessness, I often run a diagnostic test to find out which aspects of their life are troubling them. When we feel low, we can tend to think absolutely everything is going badly, but a simple diagnostic test can pinpoint what is working well and what needs attention. It is incredibly helpful to get a more precise picture of what you need to do in order to change your life.

We carry out the test by examining the four key aspects of happiness/unhappiness, and rating where the client feels they are on a scale of 1 (unhappy) to 10 (happy) in relation to each aspect:

1. relationship to loved ones, family and friends
2. meaning in work/purpose in life
3. your physical and intellectual worlds
4. your level of agency, i.e. how much you believe you have the power to change your life.

The best way to show you how to run your own diagnostic test is to show you examples from two of my own clients with whom I used this tool.

MARC
When Marc came to see me, he was thirty-three years old and married.

Relationships: 3/10
I'm a 3 because I really don't enjoy being in my family's company. I'm the eldest of three, but the other two seem to really get on. I never really enjoyed their company. I'm sporty and enjoy playing games and they were never like that. They were more into academic things, so we never had much in common. I hate family occasions. I'm always counting down the time until I can leave. I feel like the other two go out of their way to show me how much they like each other. They recently went on holiday together and never invited me, that hurt. But I wouldn't have gone if they'd asked. But it still hurt. My partner tells me I should try harder with them but the way I see it, they don't try with me either.

I know it sounds childish, but I just don't enjoy being around them. When I came out, they really weren't very supportive. My youngest brother sent a disgusting message on our family WhatsApp group about being gay, and I've never really forgiven him. He apologized and deleted it quickly, said it was meant for a friend, but what sort of person does that? You can't choose your family and all that.

My parents didn't help things. They always compared us: I was sporty and they were clever. I was clever too, but my parents never saw that. I do resent my parents for not promoting our relationship. We all had to fight for their love. It was awful. When my dad died, things got worse. I did his eulogy, but I could tell my youngest brother was angry with that. He always resented me, for some reason. My other brother always played us against each other. He tried to be all things to each of us. He was always fake!

So, that's why I'm a 3. I would obviously like a better relationship with my brothers.

I don't have many friends in my adult life. It would be nice to have someone to call up and meet and go for a pint. But I don't trust them, I think they talk about me a lot, so I just stay away from that toxicity. Having said that, they do call me up when they want advice, and that can be nice. But in general, we don't get on.

My relationship with my partner could be better. We have drifted apart in recent years. We're not as intimate as we once were, and this upsets me. I guess that's just long-term relationship stuff, but I wish it was better.

Meaning/purpose in life: 8/10

I'm a physiotherapist. I really love my work. I always wanted to work in this area, so I feel very grateful to have that opportunity. Some days I'm a 10, some days a little less because it can be very demanding. But overall, I'm an 8. I'd like to build my own practice. Working with the HSE can be too demanding and a little dysfunctional. Some days, I could see fifteen clients and then all the paperwork, I might not get home until 9.00 p.m.

Physical/intellectual world: 6/10

I don't work out enough. I know I feel better when I do, and it has always been an important part of my life, but in recent years I haven't been doing as much I would like, and it impacts on how I feel. I'm a 6 because I still work out, just not as much as I would like. I would also like to be contributing more to the field of physiotherapy. I used to write articles about my practice, but I stopped that when I became a clinical specialist. I miss it. I've always enjoyed writing.

Agency – power to effect change: 4/10

I sometimes don't know what I need to do to change how I am feeling. I often find myself daydreaming about things being different, but I don't really know what that would look like, or how I could make that change. It seems insurmountable sometimes.

OLIVIA

When Olivia came to see me, she was a forty-six-year-old GP with three children.

Relationships: 2/10

I would say I'm a 2 out of 10. I don't really feel connected to anything at the moment. My husband is a doctor, building up his private practice. I know that this is important to secure our future, but we just haven't been intimate in a long time. My kids are now in the teenage years and they don't really have much interest in being with me. Of course, I know that's normal, but I just feel so lonely. I have good friends but we're all so busy and I don't want to say how I'm feeling. I have a good relationship with my siblings but they're all so busy and my parents are elderly. I never thought I'd feel like this. I had the perfect family, but things seem like they're falling apart. We don't even have dinner together. I don't recognize my family.

Meaning/purpose in life: 7/10

I love the work I do. I'm a GP, it's demanding, but I love working with people. I have very few holidays and it can be too demanding, so that's why I'm missing 3 points here.

Physical and intellectual worlds: 5/10

I used to love swimming and playing tennis but I haven't done either of those since my husband changed direction and started his own private practice. I loved going to concerts and plays but we don't have any time. I also started the menopause this year, and I think that has had a big impact on my mental health.

Agency: 3/10

I don't know how to change things at the moment. I'm stuck in a rut and I don't know how to get out of it. My husband doesn't get home every night until 8.00 p.m. and he is exhausted. So, things don't seem like they are going to change any time soon.

What you can do

We often construct complicated interventions to manage the family we grew up in. Think about your own family. Did you have to construct a protective self that might have got in your own way? If that self was dismantled, who would you see?

Now, do the four aspects rating exercise yourself. Write a detailed account, as above, of why you chose each score.

From doing this simple exercise you can really become precise in your understanding of what needs to change in your life. But be aware that becoming the person you were meant to be takes work. You first of all have to figure out what aspects of your life need to be improved. When you don't have that clear in your mind, it can be difficult to move out of the place you are in.

It is vitally important that you track your happiness. When things are going well, ask yourself, where are you on the scale? If it has improved, ask yourself, what are you doing currently that is moving the gauge? Then, simple as it sounds, do more of that. And do less of the things that make you unhappy. Change isn't easy, but when you choose to change, and choose what that change will be, you are taking responsibility for your own happiness. What an empowering thing to do.

We all become stuck at times. It can seem like you are bobbing about in a vast ocean, no horizon in sight, desperately looking around for some sign of where to go. Getting a more precise understanding, and moving towards where you want to be, is working in the interest of your future self. In today's world of instant gratification, this process can seem a little slow, but it takes time and effort to achieve happiness and fulfilment.

YOUR GENOGRAM

Go back to your genogram. Earlier, I introduced you to the idea that you might have a fear of thriving. Write in what thriving would look like for you. Now, ask yourself the following questions.

1. What are the obstacles to achieving what you have described? Write them in.
2. How could you tackle those obstacles? Write those ideas in, too.

PART NINE

Home is Where You Start From . . . But it Doesn't Have to be Where You Finish

LOOKING BACK ON A DYSFUNCTIONAL CHILDHOOD IS VERY DIFFI-cult. I meet so many clients who really don't want to revisit the past. They remind me of myself in my twenties, desperately hoping that it would all just be consigned to the dark recesses of my mind and I could move on. Of course, moving away from our childhood experiences is an important step on the journey to self-discovery. We are not what happened to us, but who we choose to become. But we do need to deal with what happened in our early formative journey, and work through it, so that we can re-author the negative narrative about what those experiences mean.

For me, looking back is to see the utter waste of potential. We could have had a wonderful childhood and family life. My father was fun, exciting, clever, strong. He was spontaneous, didn't really care about authority, which was very exciting as children to experience. We used to play the guitar together, write songs, my mother providing the harmony. My grandmother inside her little room, watching *Glenroe* on a Sunday evening. At times, it all functioned normally. I think that was why I didn't want to look back. It was far too complicated for me to analyse, in those early days. If it had all just been awful, I think it would have been easier to process.

As I got older and gained distance from it, though, it kept coming back up. That's the problem with memory, it's not so easily defeated. One evening, as myself and my wife were talking about starting a family, I realized that I needed to start the process of healing my early childhood experience. This was 2009, and it had been ten years since I'd last spoken to my father. My last interaction with him was that fight where I'd knocked him down. I wasn't proud of that. It haunted my dreams.

Ten long winters had passed. I find that hard to comprehend. The idea that my children could be out there in the world and I would not know what was going on with them. I still can't comprehend that. There wouldn't be a wall big enough to stop me scaling it to get to my children. I remember watching the movie *Warrior* about a year or two later, where Nick Nolte plays a father seeking redemption for being an aggressive drunk and absent father to his two boys. His son aggressively denies his father's attempt at reconciliation. Nolte's character asks for forgiveness, only to be asked,

'Where were you when it mattered?' He has no reply. What struck me about this scene was that I felt so strongly for the father's position. I desperately wanted Tom Hardy's character to forgive his father and allow him back into his life. I cried watching that scene.

My father never made such overtures. In fact, he never said sorry. I think I knew he never would. So, if I was going to go back into that childhood and try to meet my father again, I knew I had to manage my expectations. I got his number from my uncle and I sent him a message. He seemed happy that I had reached out to him, and we arranged to meet in the Shelbourne one afternoon in June 2009.

I was nervous walking into the lobby. I walked through the bar and then back into the lobby and into the little area for afternoon tea, but he wasn't there. I went back into the bar, that's where I expected to find him. Again, he wasn't there. I was looking for a big, strong, good-looking man, but when I looked again, I saw a small, frail man reading the newspaper. 'Richard?' he said as I approached. He was obviously as unsure as I was. That was so incredibly upsetting, that you could pass your own father and not recognize him. Many years earlier – I must have been about fifteen – I was walking down Patrick Street in Cork and I passed him. We both just nodded at each other like strangers and walked on. I still think about that. What was he thinking? I never felt like I knew him. That was a very strange moment.

The conversation in the Shelbourne didn't yield a cathartic moment. He wasn't contrite or sorry for what had happened. When I asked him why he had been so aggressive with his children, he answered, 'It wasn't all bad.' I resigned myself to the fact that I wasn't going to have that redemptive moment I had hoped for.

I became aware that his girlfriend – the woman he had left my mother for and whose existence he had denied to my face, the other party in the affair he had blamed me for – was sitting in the corner of the room. I had to control my anger.

I remembered back to years earlier. One evening, I came home and the phone was ringing. I could tell my grandmother was bothered and upset. She was on her own and explained that the phone wouldn't stop ringing. I answered. I could tell there was someone there, but they didn't respond. I hung up and went upstairs to get ready for the night out. The phone rang again. I answered. No one spoke, but I could hear breathing. And then the voice spoke, 'Is that you, Shane?' I immediately knew whose voice it was. I recognized her because she'd rung our house before, looking for my father. I hung up.

I clearly remember my grandmother standing in the hall, upset, asking, 'Is that who I think it is?' I told her not to worry, she wouldn't be calling here again. I rang for a taxi and went straight to her house.

It is still a scene I recall with embarrassment and regret. I was no more than twenty years old, standing there, banging on her front door, shouting at her to come out. Her neighbours came out to see what all the commotion was about. Her son opened the door. I felt terrible for bringing this to his door. His mother came out and I always remember what she said because it shocked me that my father had been talking about me with her and what he said. 'Be careful,' she said to her son, 'that's Richard, his youngest. He's wild and capable of doing anything.' Was that how my father spoke about me? I have often thought about those words and imagined my father talking about me like that. I felt incredibly betrayed by him.

Now, here she was, sitting in the Shelbourne, watching me interact with my father. I was in my early thirties now and had worked out most of those early experiences. I had grown up. I was a different person. I have thought about her children a lot over the course of my life. I didn't want to think about them, but I did. And I hoped they'd also learned how to thrive.

I let the conversation with my father end naturally, and then I left. I didn't speak to him again for another four years. I walked through those revolving doors of the Shelbourne so I could confront my childhood. I was desperate to figure it out before I had children. I didn't want to carry any of that negative stuff into my children's life. I didn't want them to see aggression. I didn't want them to see a man disappointed with life, or who saw himself as a victim. I wanted to build, not destroy.

I knew I had the potential to be like him. We all did. But I used that awareness to refuse to allow that experience to play out in my adult life. It would have been the easiest thing in the world, to take on his behaviours and pass them on to my children – much easier than striving to be a good parent. But I wouldn't allow it to be present in my life, so it stopped with me. Revisiting childhood experiences and working them out is essential because it is you working in the interest of your future self. That experience in the Shelbourne, though not what I'd hoped for, was one of the most important moments in my life. All of that toxic stuff that I'd held on to, that had haunted me, dissipated that day and left me. All the anger I'd had for my father was gone.

I was sitting with my father recently, when he was sick. Time had done its thing and here we were, two very changed people with very different life paths. I felt the loss of his life, the tragic loss of all that wonderful potential, but also the incredible richness of my life. I had worked in the interest of myself many years ago and now here was future me, arrived at last, reaping the benefits. I was sitting in the hospital, with my daughter, supporting my sick father. I was no longer angry, closed off from people, living out a narrative created by others and foisted on me and my life. I had created my own narrative, a healthier one, a more authentic one. I was entirely me.

19. Accept your past self, change your present self

You will have noticed by now that all of the chapters of this book have a common thread: the recurring motif of metamorphosis. Change. Clients who come to me do so because they feel stuck, unable to change how their life is playing out in front of them. Feeling powerless about how your life is unfolding is one of the most disturbing experiences we have as adults. We are always capable of change, no matter what age we are. I meet so many clients in their late thirties and early forties who feel it is too late for them to change. But that is just an error in their thinking. Life expectancy is increasing all the time and those old, anachronistic ideas about the phases of life are no longer fit for purpose. The truth is, we can change at any time. We all have the power to change how we act, how we are perceived, and how we perceive ourselves.

Your past self

It is an interesting statistic that 47.2 years has been found to be the age when we are most unhappy. Why is that? Well, our mid-forties can be a time of deep disquiet. In the average cycle of a modern human life, early forties is when your life is more complicated than ever before: you are likely to be very serious about your career, or in the process of changing career; you might be juggling a job and studying; you might be married; you might have become a parent; you might be worrying about your health and the health of your ageing parents. Your responsibilities are greater, while the opportunities to live by your own designs and whims have decreased. And of course your hormones have started on their merry decline, so that's having an impact as well.

This is generally a time when we review our lives, look back at what we've achieved, where we're at, and where we'd like to go next. Looking back is such an important part of looking forward.

We cannot move forward into who we are meant to become without honestly looking back and re-evaluating our experience. We all came out of messy families, so looking back and understanding the impact all that mess had on your life and behaviour as an adult is an important first step in moving forward. Understanding what influenced your development, and the person you became, is significant if you want your future self to thrive. When you look back, you can become troubled by what you find, but when you realize that your parents came up in a messy family too and might not have had the tools to meet your needs, then you can start to let go.

Accepting what happened to you and letting it go can be a significant cathartic moment of gaining power in your life. We must all look back but, more importantly, we must all look forward and have an image of who we want to become. This is a good thing – it encourages you to do an honest assessment of yourself and your happiness. And from that, change can flow. It helps greatly to see this time of disquiet as a time of transition, when you are choosing what matters most, assessing where you want to put your energies, and identifying if you are living your authentic self. This is a chance to think back with the benefit of distance, to reassess, to let go of the things that are preventing you from thriving, to bring into your life more of the things that make you thrive. If you can see change as a hugely positive force, you can embrace it and make it work for you.

—

CASE STUDY
The girl who was a ghost

Rebecca came to see me because she had just come out of a two-year relationship that wasn't very healthy. She was thirty-two and felt trapped in her life. She had experienced a series of bad relationships in her twenties and was despairing about the chances of meeting someone and having a family. She had seen many therapists over the course of her life. Her older sister had died from a brain tumour when she was thirteen and Rebecca was nine, causing huge trauma to the family. Her parents had become withdrawn through grief. Rebecca often described feeling like a ghost in the house after her sister died. She viewed herself as a victim of circumstances, and felt she'd been dealt a very bad hand.

REBECCA: Things haven't been good for a long time.

RICHARD: On a scale of 10 being really happy and 1 being very unhappy, where are you?

REBECCA: A consistent 2.

RICHARD: What causes you to be a 2?

REBECCA: Oh, everything. I can't seem to do anything right. Nothing works out for me.

RICHARD: Can you explain what you feel you are not doing right?

REBECCA: Well, I keep picking losers for partners. Just go from one bad relationship to the next. Had a boyfriend when I was in college who beat me up. That's the kind of fella I go for, apparently.

RICHARD: I'm sorry to hear you had that experience, but you couldn't have known starting out that he was like that. Why do you blame yourself for his terrible behaviour?

REBECCA: I've always felt like I was at fault for everything. It's like my default position.

RICHARD: What else do you feel responsible for?

REBECCA: I know this isn't true, but I always felt kind of responsible for my sister's death. I don't know exactly how I'm responsible, but I've felt it. Maybe not responsible exactly, but it should have been me, not her. She was much better than me.

RICHARD: Can I ask you what happened to your sister?

REBECCA: She died at thirteen from a brain tumour.

RICHARD: I'm very sorry. How do you think that experience shaped your life?

REBECCA: My parents fell apart. I became a ghost in the house. It was like I died, too, in some way.

RICHARD: When you say a ghost, can you describe that further?

REBECCA: They were so consumed with their grief, they no longer saw me. I was a shadow. I remember one morning my parents came into the kitchen, I was eating Cheerios, I remember that because I just kept looking at them, moving them around, watching the milk go into the hole. My father had forgotten to do something my mother had asked him the night before and she said, 'Why can't you do the smallest thing? I don't ask you for much.' He turned around and told her to fuck off and leave him alone. I kept my head down, in the cereal, they both just left the house fighting. They forgot they had to bring me to school. I was left sitting there, looking at the cereal. I felt like things weren't real. Like I wasn't even there. They didn't come back. I just went back to bed and cried. Why did that have to happen to us? My parents were good people. Why did that happen to me?

RICHARD: When you think those thoughts, what conclusion do you come to?

REBECCA: I'm cursed.

RICHARD: That must feel very powerless?

REBECCA: I am powerless. I can't change what happened. I have to live with it every day. (*She is very upset and crying.*) It's just not fair.

RICHARD: Can I ask you what your sister's name is?

REBECCA: Rachel.

RICHARD: Do you remember her well?

REBECCA: That's another thing, I really worry that I'll forget her. Sometimes I wake up unable to breathe because I think I've forgotten the sound of her voice.

RICHARD: Sounds like you really love your sister.

REBECCA: She was so beautiful. I know she was only a child, but she was very mature for her age. An old soul.

RICHARD: If she was here sitting next to you today, what do you think she would say to you?

REBECCA: Live your life and stop dating losers.

RICHARD: When she says live your life, what is she speaking to?

REBECCA: I have a terrible tendency to live in the past.

RICHARD: What do you mean?

REBECCA: I guess, I feel like my childhood fucked me up and impacted every aspect of my life. I think I can't really function as an adult.

RICHARD: Up to this point, how have those thoughts helped you?

REBECCA: They really haven't.

RICHARD: So let's say, six sessions from now, you leave the clinic thinking, 'Wow, that really helped, I feel much better' – what would be different in your life?

REBECCA: I would stop blaming my childhood and start living my life.

RICHARD: What needs to happen for that to happen?

REBECCA: I know I have to take responsibility for my life.

RICHARD: What gets in the way of that?

REBECCA: Those negative thoughts.

RICHARD: Is there some comfort in those thoughts?

REBECCA: I've never thought about it like that, but I guess there is comfort in them in some way.

RICHARD: In what way?

REBECCA: Things are beyond my control. It's not my fault my life is a mess.

RICHARD: Whose fault is it?

REBECCA: I'm not saying it's Rachel's fault, but her death caused so much trauma. And my parents' reaction to it. We still don't talk about it. It's all so terrible. Why did it have to happen to us? We were a happy family.

RICHARD: Do you think about God in those moments?

REBECCA: There can't be a God, or if there is, fuck him or whatever he/she is.

RICHARD: You're angry with God?

REBECCA: Yes, very angry.

RICHARD: What would you like to ask God, if you could?

REBECCA: Why us?

RICHARD: What do you think the response would be?

REBECCA: I don't know, that it just happened. No reason to it.

RICHARD: Would that mean you're not cursed?

REBECCA: Maybe.

RICHARD: And what would it mean if you did have control over your life and it's not cursed?

REBECCA: I'd have to take responsibility for myself.

RICHARD: What do you want your life to be like, I mean, how would you know it's going well?

REBECCA: Meet a decent guy, start a family, get control of my life, stop looking for excuses for why it's not the way I want it to be.

RICHARD: Would that be a way to honour Rachel? To live your life fully?

REBECCA: Yes.

—

It is impossible to move through this world without experiencing some degree of suffering and pain. It is a fundamental part of the human condition. If we accept this, it means we take suffering as a normal part of the human experience, and that means we will not allow ourselves to feel victimized when it occurs to us. We cannot be victims when something is a normal part of life experience. Some people endure unspeakable tragedies in life. Sometimes, people are the victim of a malevolent perpetrator. But it doesn't have to define us. You are far more than what happened to you.

Victor Frankl, a man who experienced incomprehensible suffering at the hands of the Nazi terror machine, said:

'Everything can be taken from a man but one thing: the last of the human freedoms – to choose one's attitude in any given set of circumstances.'

The power to choose your response to what happened in your life is the greatest power you have. You can choose to use it as an excuse for why you are unhappy, which will manifest pervasive sorrow and suffering into your life, or you can be resolute and decide to stride out there into the world and, in doing so, allow yourself the opportunity to succeed.

—

CASE STUDY
The ghost who became more solid

Rebecca, who had previously described herself as 'a ghost' – a victim of tragic circumstances in her childhood, who was powerless to change her life – had gained some valuable insights in her sessions with me. I was keen to see if she had been able to apply them in her daily interactions.

RICHARD: How are things going since I last saw you, Rebecca?

REBECCA: Actually, a bit better, I feel more solid.

RICHARD: What do you mean?

REBECCA: I feel more like myself. I've really started doing that thing you said about listening to myself as if I'm a stranger, and things have changed a lot.

RICHARD: Okay, so you did that little exercise I gave you about listening to how you speak to yourself, as if you were a stranger, and what have you noticed?

REBECCA: Jesus, I'm a moany bitch.

RICHARD: Not quite the conclusion I was hoping you'd come to.

REBECCA (*laughing*): No, but maybe the truth.

RICHARD: So what has that conclusion meant for you?

REBECCA: Stop moaning. I met a friend recently and she even noticed the change in me.

RICHARD: What did she say to show she noticed a change?

REBECCA: It was really interesting because she said, 'You seem like your old self.'

RICHARD: I wonder what she saw to introduce her to that old self?

REBECCA: I think it was because I was joking with her about things and looking forward to the weekend and heading out with friends.

RICHARD: On the scale of 1 to 10, where are you
  currently?

REBECCA: 6 or 7.

RICHARD: What has changed from being a 2?

REBECCA: I have been thinking about this a lot. I think what
  has helped me is understanding that I am responsible for
  my happiness, that no one is going to give it to me. And
  something you said really stuck in my head – you asked
  me about honouring Rachel. I think I was dishonouring
  her with who I was being. I was taking my life for
  granted. I think about that every morning I wake up
  now: how will I honour Rachel today? And it's just
  about living in a better way. That's what Rachel would
  have wanted. That's what I want.

—

Forgive and let go

Forgiveness is such a huge concept, and people often really struggle
with it. They can feel that to forgive the person who hurt them is to
give away their power or to let that person off the hook. But for me,
seeing people in all their complexity, their humanity, their fears, their
failed solutions, breaks down the narrow lens through which we
have viewed them. We can so easily reduce people to the neat roles
of villain or hero. But people are more complicated than that. I
thought my father was the villain in my early life, but he no longer
holds that title. He never was the villain, but a human being who was
struggling. He bullied us at times, made us feel small, physically and
intellectually. He used to refer to me sarcastically as the 'dark poet',
to try to get a response from me in an argument. Which it always
did. But those memories don't dominate my thoughts now. They're
in there, but I have moved beyond them as a source of power in my
life. Understanding that my father was a human being who struggled really helped me to work through some of those negative
feelings. It helped me to forgive him and start my healing process.

That day in the Shelbourne, I went to see my father so that I would not be bitter and resentful of him as I moved into parenthood. I wanted to forgive him so that I could thrive. I was thinking of my future self. I didn't want him to die and our last contact to have been a physical fight. I didn't want to have to deal with that later in my life. I was seeing him again on my terms, for my benefit.

I think it's often the case that people view 'letting go' as a process whereby the thing they've been holding on to is prised off them and drifts away, leaving them alone. I have watched many people go through the process of letting go, and I don't see it like that. I see them prise their hands off the negative memory or interpretation that they have been holding on to and leave it behind, allowing themselves to steer towards the shore they want to live on, the better place. You have to let go – then you'll be free.

What you can do

We can come to view forgiveness as weakness or letting someone who hurt us remain unaccountable for their actions. But I have seen in my clinic, and in my personal life, the power forgiveness has to heal internal scars. Sometimes our thinking is clouded by emotion and it prevents us from moving forward.

Think about what it would mean to forgive someone who has hurt you. Would it help to see them fully, from their childhood to adulthood? Going back to your genogram might help with this process. Look at all the things that had an impact on them to become who they were and how they acted as parents.

The aim here is not to excuse or forget, it is to see and understand and let go. In Chapter 9 ('Comfortably numb – the power of positive feedback loops') I described the tight fist, holding it closed so tightly it's painful. Letting go is like opening your fist, so that it no longer keeps a death grip on your past. It's over. Let it go.

Change your present self

You'll recall from Chapter 15 ('Positive relations') the Jungian concept of the circumambulation of the self. This tells us that change is a series of forward movements interspersed with backward movements: one step forward, two steps back, as the saying goes. Change does not happen in a straight line, and we can fall back into old habits. This is because, as you begin to change, your brain will do everything to push you back to what is familiar, to your old thoughts and habits. We have more than 60,000 thoughts a day, and nearly 90 per cent of those are what we thought yesterday. We are creatures of habit – that's our comfort zone. That means you only have about a 10 per cent chance of change happening organically, without your intentional intervention.

There is a famous saying in neuroscience: 'Neurons that fire together wire together.' This explains how we come to think in a particular way – and see it as the only way. When we are young and the brain's plasticity is significantly more malleable, the story we hear about ourselves gets written. When we learn something new, synapses connect, so our brain literally changes with new information. Billions of neurons fire when we are thinking, which is all the time. The more we think a thought, the more those neurons connect. Once they start to connect, all the other potential thoughts fade.

Once we repeat a thought and find confirmation, it becomes a pathway. It's like an algorithm: the more you watch a particular video, the stronger the algorithm gets, and all other potential videos disappear. Similarly, the more you think something, the more the neural growth factor knits around that thought, which means all the other thoughts never get a chance to be heard. This can cause an incredible amount of distress as we get caught thinking in negative patterns. We might even know that a thought isn't correct, but we still think it. We are running a neural circuit loop, and it takes over.

Changing the way you think means rewiring those neurons that fired many years ago. Once you do that, you can do anything.

Once you've got past yourself, you'll have to get past the people close to you, who are used to you being a particular way or who are comfortable with the label they have attached to you. The beliefs of others significantly shape the beliefs we hold about ourselves, which impacts on how we behave and how we feel. Changing and being true to ourselves will disrupt others and the beliefs they have come to hold about us. If you are going to grow and change, you will have to get comfortable with the discomfort of others.

As we found out in Chapter 7 ('How you can get sacrificed for family balance'), families crave balance. When you disrupt that balance by trying to change yourself, family members might resist the change. This is because the label you were assigned contributed to an important equilibrium in your family. Do not be surprised or disheartened if your attempts at change are resisted, or when you go back into your family that you fall back into those earlier ideas about who you are. Expect it, understand what it is. They will attempt to push you back into what is familiar and comfortable for them. You might also do it to yourself. But you must hold your ground, be true to yourself and resist this.

We are not islands, we all came from complicated family systems with parents who navigated their own complicated family systems. But we do have power to re-author any life experience we have had. It took me some years to figure that out. I was always fearful I'd turn into my father. I drank heavily in my twenties, like everyone else in my peer group, and it brought me into some dangerous situations. I was always aware of the person I dated and what their personality was like. I realized very early on that I needed to meet someone who could be the counterpoint to my negative childhood experiences and who would be a solid ally in life.

That choice in partner was really the starting point of pulling myself out of some negative habits. But I also evaluated what was working in my life and what was impeding my progress. Slowly, I started to remove the negative behaviours, until I couldn't remember what they were. It took work, because of the family I came up in, my position in that family and the attachment type I experienced, but it wasn't impossible, and I did change. I was no longer the sullen, wild, irascible, frightened kid I had been for so long. I cultivated positive personality traits, worked on being more extraverted and open to people, I started to trust people (that was probably the hardest) and I started to tell myself that I was worthy of someone's love. The more I opened up, the more life opened up, and I started to see myself clearly.

What you can do
Ask yourself three important questions.

- Who do I want to be?
- What do I want people to say about the kind of person I am?
- What is getting in the way of manifesting that person into reality?

Don't be afraid of the answers. When you start living authentically, things will change dramatically. You lose that old fake persona and you gain truth, an authentic sense of self. What a wonderful gift to give yourself.

YOUR GENOGRAM ·

We have now completed a very detailed picture of your family of origin and your own family.

1. On your genogram, write next to your name the changes you think you need to make in your life, to improve it.
2. Choose one change per month and track it over that month.

Remember, people often attempt to change too much and become disillusioned very quickly. Don't let this happen to you after all your hard work.

20.   *Write your own life story*

Our lives are shaped and defined by the stories we create about them. There is nothing as important as the story you tell yourself about who you are and what you are capable of. That voice in your head, narrating yourself to you, is powerful, and you live by its interpretation of what happened, how you handled it, and who you have become. If that voice is constantly whispering negatives, it is dragging you down, writing a story in which you are the downtrodden one, the broken one, the one who messes up or is messed up, the one who cannot succeed.

Neuroscience explains that when we think about ourselves, our thoughts are indistinguishable from negative feelings. That means we can easily arrive at the conclusion that we are 'losers', 'pathetic', 'unlovable', 'helpless', 'weak', et cetera. Once we start to write the story of our life like this, we lose our sense of agency. Those external forces, such as attachment style, family of origin, position in that family, negative family legacy, labelling, all crowd into the narrative and rewrite it – and we feel powerless to prevent that.

The work of David Epston and Michael White, an anthropologist and a social worker, introduced the concept of narrative therapy into the therapeutic field. One of the key aspects of their work was to illuminate how stories, or interpretations of events, shape people's identities. We are a complicated story, with many narratives and sub-narratives that can be rewritten at any time.

When you view your life through the narrative lens, you begin to see that you can view the problem separately from yourself. In Michael White's words, 'the person is not the problem, the problem is the problem'. This can be a very liberating thing to realize. It's so easy to view yourself as the problem. But if you thought about it like this instead, putting distance between yourself and the problem, what would change? Maybe you would gain more agency over what has been troubling you, because you now understand that *you* are not the problem, that the problem is the problem, and you only have to tackle the problem, not disassemble and rebuild your entire self to solve the problem.

Epston and White developed four elements that need to be explored when analysing the storyline of a person's life:

1. events . . .
2. in a sequence . . .
3. across time . . .
4. organized according to a plot or theme (generally negative).

This is how you tell yourself the story of you: by selecting certain events that are deemed to be evidence of who/what you are, putting them together into a sequential narrative across your lifetime, which means you're *definitely*, *always* like this – and that becomes the 'theme' of your life and of you, and that theme is very often negative. So you might tell yourself, 'Well, I'm just hopeless at relationships, look at this event and that memory and that terrible outcome. I'm always like this. It's just who I am. Always was. Impossible to change. I'll never find love.'

You will have to consider each of those four elements when rewriting your life story. Events happen in all of our lives that we have no power over. We will all experience suffering to varying degrees as we move through life. But it is how we come to interpret those life events that will make the difference between collapsing under the weight of them or moving through them. How we write or describe the events that happen to us is massively important. And at the heart of it is that core idea: the problem is separate from the person. You are not the problem, the problem is not you; they are two separate things that have overlapped for a time and affected each other.

That degree of separation gives us perspective and allows us to exist beyond our experiences. And, more importantly, it allows us to thrive outside of them.

CASE STUDY
The bottomless pit of self-blame

I had a client who had been ripped off by his business partner. He started with nothing and built a very successful private law firm and was proud of this achievement. However, his partner had a gambling problem and had stolen a considerable amount of the firm's money, leaving him in a difficult situation and having to rebuild the firm again.

In our first session, he was visibly shaken by this event. As his story unfolded, it was very clear that he was constantly berating himself over this. He spoke about his intuition, how he'd had a feeling something was wrong but had ignored it. He authored that as weakness and a desire to be liked – both personal failings.

During his analysis we went back to his childhood. He told me he wasn't liked as a kid and spent most lunch breaks on his own, feeling pathetic. His law firm had represented a new narrative in his life: it was successful and he was well regarded in his field. He'd hired his business partner because he'd known him in college and had always wanted to impress him. He spoke about this man in glowing terms, and talked about himself with self-loathing and despair. He hadn't even been able to bring himself to tell his wife yet, and he described that as weakness and a lack of 'backbone'.

In his mind, the success of his firm had become an anomaly in his pathetic life story. It was a confusing outlier in an otherwise failed life. His take on what had happened and why was causing him deep despair and anguish. He said he had been experiencing suicidal ideation. This one event was collapsing everything around him.

In truth, everything in his life hadn't collapsed. He had lost money, but that was all. In our first conversation, we established that the amount stolen was significant but wouldn't sink the firm. The firm would survive. We discussed how the true damage was his being taken advantage of and not listening to his inner voice – those elements of the story were having a profound impact on his sense of self. He had authored this event as an example of how useless he was and how nobody ever respected him. He had over-written the important story of how he had built such an incredible practice that it could withstand the devious machinations of an addict colleague.

Over the course of the sessions, we looked at different events where people had been taken advantage of, questioning whether we should blame the victim or the perpetrator. Slowly, we started to free him from the destructive narrative he had constructed for himself. He didn't know his colleague had been stealing from the firm because he'd trusted him, not because he was pathetic and useless. He stopped viewing himself as that child no one liked and began to narrate a different story about overcoming a criminal event in his practice. It took some time for him to move beyond his almost concrete narrative about being pathetic, but eventually he did. And he began to thrive again.

His ability to get over this setback and thrive was the direct result of rewriting that life event in a new, more accurate narrative. Once he did that, he was able to move on in his life.

—

We all develop a narrative about who we are, what we are about, and what we are capable of. But that story has had many writers, some of whom misunderstood the protagonist, so the story became corrupted along the way. None of us starts off thinking we are weak, vulnerable and unlovable. We develop those negative and untrue ideas as we move through life and we internalize the feedback and experiences we have had on that sinuous journey. If I asked you what part of your story do you like, what would you say? And if I asked you what part do you dislike, what would you say? And what would happen if this element was removed from your story? Would you start to thrive?

We have told ourselves the story of who we are for so long, we perceive it as the undeniable truth. But it is not the single truth of the matter. It is a version of events, and it is a narrative waiting to be re-authored.

What you can do

Think of a dominant story you tell yourself about who you are. Remember what I said: thoughts about self-consciousness are indistinguishable from negative emotions, so we are primed to think negatively about ourselves. That's the first realization in re-authoring your story. It is extremely likely that you have written the story negatively, and now you can write it in a more positive way.

First, write out that dominant story as you tell it to yourself.

Now, start to question it. Ask a question that would contradict its veracity. What gets in the way of you telling this dominant story in a more positive way?

Read the story again – where you have negative words, such as 'powerless', 'weak', 'useless', 'typical', could you swap in neutral or positive words instead? If your friend told you the same story, how would you try to help them re-author it? You'd cut them some slack, wouldn't you? You'd look at their motives and actions from different angles. Do that for yourself now. Write in the new words over the negative words.

How does your story read now? Is the story false, or is it simply bringing in more viewpoints and possibilities?

How would your life start to look, if you did this for all of the stories you tell about yourself?

YOUR GENOGRAM

For your final genogram, I want you to look at the 'map' of your life that you have created – and appreciate your efforts in going to that trouble for yourself.

1. Look at all the information you have recorded, and really hear what it is saying about who you are and who you want to be.
2. Look at the dominant story you just re-authored and how it changes your perspective on that life experience.

That is the function of the genogram – to give you perspective on who you are and what you are capable of. Use that to start living in the ways that help you to thrive.

Epilogue

A last thought – almost zero

Let me take you on a journey.

Imagine, for a moment, the story of your mother and father, how they met and how they set you going. What do you think the odds were of you being born? Well, according to scientific research, the chances that your father met your mother are about 1 in 20,000. Think for a moment of all the people your parents met before they came together. Scientists argue that they would have met approximately 10,000 people before they met each other. Now, think of all the places they travelled to, all the conversations they had with new, exciting people from around the world. With every new connection, the odds of you being born shifted. Remember the photograph in *Back to the Future*? Every time your father chatted to someone with smooth indifference, made one of his little jokes, or every time your mother went to the cinema with a potential suitor, pushed her hair behind her ears, revealing her dimples, your odds got longer and longer.

They did meet, and they did get together. But that is only the start of the journey. The chances of your parents hitting it off enough to have offspring are about 1 in 40 million. Not great odds, but not impossible. I'm an optimist.

This is where things get serious. You are the product of one sperm connecting with one egg. Due to the process of meiosis, each egg and each sperm are genetically unique. A fertile woman produces around 100,000 eggs over the course of her reproductive life. A man produces over 12 trillion sperm during the course of an average male lifespan. He won't need all of them, perhaps a third, which is 4 trillion. Now, the chances of one sperm that has half your little face on it, hitting one egg, with the other half of your little face on it, is about 1 in 400 quadrillion.

That's just the odds for your parents and you. If we stretch the journey back further, we go right back through evolution to figure out the odds of you being the product of an unbroken lineage that connects back to the start of human life on Earth. Those odds are so staggering, they are nearly incomprehensible. Dr Binazir, from Harvard University, in his calculation, concluded that to get anywhere near the correct figure, we'd have to multiple 400 quadrillion to the power of 150,000 (the number of generations of humanity that have gone before us) to get even close to the actual odds of your birth. That figure is so great, it is impossible for me to write it out here. It would take up the entire book!

Let me give you a comparison. Let's say you are travelling by plane over all the deserts on Earth and you drop a marble out of the plane. You are tasked with finding that marble, with only one attempt, while blindfolded. As you set out on your journey, blindfolded and disorientated, you reach down into the sand and pluck from the dusty depths of the desert . . . the marble! A miracle? Absolutely. A miracle defies the odds to exist. The odds of you existing are almost zero. You have defied all the odds to be sitting here reading this book. You are a miracle. It's time to start celebrating your life. All the research says this is the only life you get. I can't even bring myself to think of calculating the odds of this happening again. All evidence would say it doesn't. This is your one true miracle. Don't waste it.

This book has attempted to bring you into contact with all the invisible forces that drive your life. We are never far from our childhood, it is present in everything we do. How we were raised, the attachments we experienced in those early days, what our parents modelled for us, our personality traits, the love language we speak, all this shaped the story we tell ourselves about who we are. But it's just that, a story. And all stories can be rewritten and revised and updated.

It has been such a great privilege to go on this journey with you. I have gained more insights into my own life writing this book. Life, as the old cliché goes, is short. Our childhood has happened, we cannot change that, but we do have power over how it impacts on us in the present and the future. You have far more power than you realize, you are the agent of change. This book was designed to be a catalyst for that change.

The home is where the start is, but it isn't where we finish, that story is waiting for you to write it.

Now, get into making your miracle count.

Acknowledgements

I would like to acknowledge the incredible work of Rachel Pierce. I had the seed of an idea and Rachel gently guided me to write the book it was meant to be. Her editorial decisions enriched the content of this book.

To my agent Faith O'Grady, we sat in a coffee shop and drafted up the idea that would become this book. She's a great person to have in your corner.

I'd like to acknowledge Patricia Deevy and all of the Penguin staff who helped bring this book into the world. I have always left Patricia's company invigorated and ready to write.

I'd also like to acknowledge Esther McCarthy, the lifestyle editor with the *Irish Examiner*. Your friendship over the years has meant a lot to me. God only knows what my ego would be like without your steady, humbling presence.

To my brothers, Cian and Shane, we grew up together in this family, Cian introduced me to The Beatles (one of the best gifts I received), and Shane, we shared a room together, your love and support has been a source of light.

To my mother, your sense of humour, style and good nature have always inspired.

Finally, I have to acknowledge Erica, the girl I met in Douglas, Cork. We have been together, inseparable, laughing, supporting, building, parenting and growing up ever since. Your love never wavers, your support is absolute. You made me become a man. And to my three daughters, Hannah, Lizzy and Sophie, you guys give my life meaning.

Notes

1. Finding the patterns in your life story

p. 5 **The genogram was developed in the 1980s**: for an in-depth look at genograms, and how they are used in family therapy, see McGoldrick, M., Gerson, R. & Petry, S. 2020. *Genograms: Assessment and Treatment*. Fourth edition. New York, NY: W. W. Norton.

3. How we learn – welcome to your brain!

p. 28 **the amygdala plays a far more important role in human behaviour than simple fight-or-flight responses**: see Gray, J. A. & McNaughton, N. 2003. *The Neuropsychology of Anxiety*. Second edition. New York, NY: Oxford University Press.

p. 28 **the amygdala plays a significant role in the functioning of memory**: see Tranel, D. & Hyman, B. T. 1990. 'Neuropsychological correlates of bilateral amygdala damage'. *Archives of Neurology*, 47 (3), 349–55.

p. 35 **recent research by neuroscientist Jeff Hawkins**: see Hawkins, J. 2021. *A Thousand Brains: A New Theory of Intelligence*. New York, NY: Basic Books.

4. Family dynamics

p. 48 **close to half of all marriages today are at least second marriages for one partner**: See Gretchen Livingston, 'Four-in-Ten Couples are saying "I Do," Again: Growing Number of Adults Have Remarried'. Pew Research Center report, 14 November 2014.

p. 48 **about 16 per cent of children live in blended families**: see www. pewresearch.org/social-trends/2015/12/17/1-the-american-family-today/ (accessed February 2023).

11. *Addiction and the family*

p. 115 **The Grant Study . . . by Harvard University**: for a summary of the findings, see Liz Mineo, 'Good genes are nice, but joy is better'. *The Harvard Gazette*, 11 April 2017.

13. *The language of love*

p. 143 **speakers of different languages might view the world differently**: see Lera Boroditsky, 'How Language Shapes Thought'. *Scientific American*, 1 February 2011.

p. 146 **The concept of love languages**: see Chapman, G. 2015. *The 5 Love Languages: The Secret to Love That Lasts*. Chicago, IL: Moody Publishers.

20. *Write your own life story*

p. 229 **The work of David Epston and Michael White**: see White, M. & Epston, D. 1990. *Narrative Means to Therapeutic Ends*. New York, NY: W. W. Norton; White, M. & Epston, D. 1992. *Experience, Contradiction, Narrative & Imagination*. Selected papers of David Epston and Michael White. Australia: Dulwich Centre, Adelaide; White, M. 2001. 'Narrative practice and the unpacking of identity conclusions'. *Gecko: A Journal of Deconstruction and Narrative Ideas in Therapeutic Practice*, no. 1, 28–55.